"Irene Pritzker's approach to philanthropy is a masterclass in transformative partnerships. She invests in a way that allows organizations to adapt, evolve, and thrive in response to the shifting needs of the communities they serve. This book is vital for anyone seeking to understand how strategic funding aligned with the Sustainable Development Goals can drive systemic change."

Aashti Zaidi Hai, CEO, Global Schools Forum

"By centering local actors, Irene Pritzker and the IDP Foundation are leading a movement to challenge conventional thinking about philanthropy and development. *The School in the Market* is not only a compelling read—it is a powerful call to adopt inclusive, collaborative models that align with the interconnected goals of the SDGs. This is investing for impact in action!"

Amir Dossal, former executive director, United Nations Office for Partnerships; founder and president, Global Partnerships Forum

"As described in this book, the IDP Foundation's commitment to uplifting Ghanaians by partnering with us while deeply respecting our culture and traditions and never imposing their own beliefs or identity made them true trailblazers in the world of international development. They are still blazing trails, and the world is paying attention."

Tony Fosu, CEO, Sinapi Aba Savings & Loans

"Irene Pritzker perceived what the creators of *Sesame Street* knew: that high-quality early education can change children's lives. *The School in the Market* reveals how Pritzker's inspiration led to an innovative education program with transformative results. Sesame Workshop was proud to be a part of this work, creating teacher-training resources featuring Sesame's beloved characters that model play-based, child-centered techniques, leading to more engaged classrooms and inspiring teachers and students alike."

Sherrie Westin, president and CEO, Sesame Workshop

IRENE PRITZKER

The

SCHOOL
in the
MARKET

How Localization Is Helping Africans
Start Their Own Education Revolution

amplify

an imprint of Amplify Publishing Group

amplify

an imprint of Amplify | Publishing Group

www.amplifypublishinggroup.com

*The School in the Market: How Localization Is Helping Africans
Start Their Own Education Revolution*

For more information, please contact:
Amplify Publishing, an imprint of Amplify Publishing Group
620 Herndon Parkway, Suite 220
Herndon, VA 20170
info@amplifypublishing.com

Library of Congress Control Number: 2025911277

CPSIA Code: PRV0725A

ISBN-13: 979-8-89138-718-8

Printed in United States

For my daughter, Liesel,
and for Paulina Nlando.

Education is the most powerful weapon which you can use to change the world.

—Nelson Mandela

CONTENTS

FOREWORD

Tony Fosu, chief executive officer,
Sinapi Aba Savings & Loans

Since 2009, I have been very fortunate to be a part of an extraordinary relationship between Sinapi Aba and the IDP (Innovation, Development, and Progress) Foundation under the leadership of Irene Pritzker.

As a Ghanaian, I was fortunate to receive an excellent education—an opportunity many of my fellow citizens did not have. This privilege instilled in me a mission to help transform Ghana through education, one of the most reliable pathways to lifting a nation and its people out of poverty.

In Ghana, as in many regions of Africa, national development is significantly hindered by low literacy rates. At the time of Ghana's independence in 1957, our literacy rate and economic standing were comparable to those of South Korea. However, more recently, Ghana's literacy rate stands at approximately 79 percent (2021), while South Korea boasts an impressive 98 percent.* This stark

---

* Ghana Statistical Service, "Ghana 2021 Population and Housing Census, General Report Volume 3D: Literacy & Education," November 2021, https://statsghana.gov. gh/gssmain/fileUpload/pressrelease/2021%20PHC%20General%20Report%20

contrast is reflected in economic outcomes—South Korea's gross domestic product (GDP) per capita has surged to over US$30,000, whereas Ghana's remains around US$2,500.*

Education is a proven catalyst for upward mobility, lifting individuals from poverty into the middle and even upper class. Investing in education is not just a moral imperative; it is an economic necessity for national progress.

My own story is a good example of this. There were seven of us—five boys and two girls. I grew up in quite a poor neighborhood. My mother sold charcoal while taking care of us with the support of my father. My parents were both very concerned about ensuring that we had a quality education, and they worked incredibly hard to place us in a British school—a low-fee private school run by nuns. The school I attended made me well equipped to go to university, where I thrived.

In Ghana, when you finish university, it is mandatory to engage for a year in national service. You are usually given the option to work with a governmental institution or in community-based development organizations. I really wanted to work with a non-governmental organization (NGO), and I was posted to Sinapi Aba—a transformational microfinance organization. Sinapi's mission and vision—to ensure that the economically disadvantaged are provided with opportunities to make a dignified living for themselves—resonated with my personal aspirations and ambitions.

Vol%203D_Literacy%20and%20Education.pdf?utm; World Population Review, "Literacy Rate by Country 2025," accessed March 2025, https://worldpopulationreview.com/country-rankings/literacy-rate-by-country?utm.

* World Bank Group, "Data for Ghana, Korea, Rep.," accessed March 2025, https://data.worldbank.org/?locations=GH-KR&utm.

I fell in love with the organization from the start and excelled immediately because I was doing work that truly mattered to me. My mother was an illiterate trader, and now I was working with others just like her—teaching them how to keep basic records, build strong customer relationships, understand the difference between revenue and profit, and navigate the process of taking and repaying a loan. It was more than a job; it was a mission.

After completing my national service, I was offered the opportunity to stay. In less than a year, I was promoted to branch supervisor, then manager. From there, I moved from a small branch to a larger one, eventually rising to area manager. And in just seven years, I became CEO—leading an organization that reflected my values and my passion for empowering others.

As CEO, I had the good fortune to meet Irene Pritzker and her daughter, Liesel. They were in Ghana looking to partner with a financial institution to help bring some security and infrastructure to low-fee private schools. Most low-fee private schools in Ghana are started by entrepreneurs who recognize that the state is unable to support the educational needs of all its citizens, so they have founded schools to fill the gap. Knowing that their students will come from mostly very poor families, they must keep their fees low.

As soon as we met, I was moved by Irene and Liesel's passion to help provide children—particularly poor children—with an education. That meeting with Irene and Liesel and my subsequent collaboration with the IDP Foundation became one of the best things that ever happened to Sinapi—and to me. Our relationship and the common vision we proceeded to build together are dear to my heart. I have had a lot of other partnerships over the course of my years with Sinapi Aba, but there are none like this one.

Prior to working with the IDP Foundation, Sinapi Aba had engaged mostly with group microloans for individuals who come together to take out a loan. Under the terms of a group microloan, if one person defaults, the others absorb the cost. When Irene came to us with her proposal to loan to low-fee private schools, I jumped at the chance. She offered to guarantee that we could work directly with individuals, providing them with a financial safety net and supporting the education of some of Ghana's most vulnerable children.

Irene and Liesel were different from most Western NGO executives with whom I had previously worked. They did not stride in and tell us what to do. They did not use their money to try and make us think like them. They wanted to know what *we* wanted. They respected our perspective and our traditions. And then, yes, they provided their financial support—and so much more.

I was deeply impressed with their commitment, and my admiration only grew as we started driving around Ghana visiting schools. I asked myself: *Why would an* obroni *(white person) stray from her comfort zone in America to come here to Ghana?* It made no sense to me. Yet, clearly, she was driven. She was determined to find out how to make things that seemed impossible or impractical possible and practical.

Although I was the CEO, I jumped behind the steering wheel whenever possible during these tours. Irene would always sit in the front seat. We drove from Accra to Kumasi to Techiman to Tamale to the northernmost regions, stopping along the way to visit almost all the communities we came across. At the end of each eight- or nine-hour day, we engaged in discussions and meetings, evolving our thinking, drafting and redrafting, and strategizing and re-strategizing.

Our mission wasn't to build new schools from the ground up but to identify those already serving the most vulnerable and poorest families—schools in desperate need of support, rejuvenation, and rebuilding. We drove together from Accra almost to the border of Burkina Faso, looking for the kind of schools we wanted in our program. We stayed together in challenging environments and made sacrifices together because we believed in each other and the work we wanted to accomplish.

I was content to have my team find schools to be a part of the program, but Irene said repeatedly, "No. I want to see for myself." We drove for hours and hours at a time. Irene has made uncountable trips to Ghana and has exposed herself to numerous risks in doing so.

Meanwhile, there was Liesel. Liesel was twenty-four when she first came to Ghana. I wondered, *Why would this young woman do this? Why would she leave her education and come to help educate vulnerable Ghanaians?* Yet, she clearly wanted to be with us, and like Irene, she didn't care about risks or danger. I sometimes think, *If I were born on the other side of the globe, would I do this?* I don't know whether I would.

Irene's energy was driven by her deep passion for giving these children the chance to attend school—not just to learn, but to see a world of possibilities unfold before them. She wanted them to experience the joy of a nurturing environment, one where they felt supported and inspired to dream beyond their circumstances. This also further inspired me!

She didn't come with a model; she came with a passion, and she seemed to understand from the beginning that any program we might create needed to be culturally Ghanaian. With her passion and our knowledge of the field and terrain, we created a program together. Ghanaians have partnered in running the program from the outset. We built it, designed it, and constructed the whole concept together in Kumasi.

I was also impressed that she wanted the program to be sustainable right from the beginning. She was not interested in supporting something that would depend on aid forever. Her interest in replicability and scalability was evident right at the onset. The show of commitment from the donor who wanted to be profoundly involved has been what has distinguished this from our bank's other relationships. A check has a tangible and specific value—but the level of commitment Irene and Liesel showed is invaluable and unquantifiable.

What we designed with the IDP Foundation is not just a school's loan portfolio. It's something bigger. It is a deep bond of trust; something that no one had ever done before. And the relationship has been beneficial to us both. I want this to continue forever.

At Sinapi Aba, we are committed to creating transformation across all of Ghana. In this book, you will read about one of the most transformative programs among the many impactful initiatives that Sinapi Aba runs in Ghana. In turn, this is now having wide-reaching effects on the global stage, making Sinapi Aba known beyond Ghana, in places that we would otherwise never reach.

I am a Ghanaian and an African. The IDP Foundation's commitment to uplifting Ghanaians by partnering with us—while deeply respecting our culture and traditions and never imposing their own beliefs or identity—made them true trailblazers in the world of development. They are still blazing trails, and the world is paying attention. You should, too.

I hope you enjoy the story contained within this book and sense the adventure, hard work, excitement, respect, determination, and innovative thinking that went into creating what has turned out to be a remarkable and enduring program.

PROLOGUE

It is July 2, 2008, and I am in Accra, Ghana, walking through the Agbogbloshie Market. I am on a guided visit to Paulina's Queensland School, whose sole proprietor, Paulina Nlando, chose that name because of her belief that all the little girls who are her students could one day be queens—if they were to receive a good education.*

The market is a vast hub of wholesale and retail trade, where people put their wares out on mats. It bustles with the full spectrum of humanity. It is vibrant, filled with life, the scent of food mingled with humidity, dust, and the sweat of thousands of people.

People sleep within the market even though it is forbidden by the metropolitan authority. Tumbledown stalls selling a vast array of wares abound. There are thick, exposed electrical cables precariously

---

* This book is partly my story, but it's mostly the story of the IDP Foundation and the Rising Schools Program. It's also the story of many of the people—like Paulina—who have been deeply affected by the work of the foundation. Because some of my personal stories profoundly impacted the way the foundation was formed, the way it runs, and certainly its pioneering spirit, I have included them to provide context.

placed, creating trip hazards among the mud- and urine-soaked pathways that line the stalls. There are also many open, unprotected fires for cooking.

Scores of women carry large baskets of yams on their heads with their babies strapped to their backs. When those babies grow too big to be carried, what are the mothers to do? They certainly can't afford babysitters. Sometimes a few parents come together and contribute a little money to create a *crèche*, or nursery, which grows into a primary school. In fact, community members frustrated with the lack of a functional primary school often start their own schools, and it is one of those I am going to visit today.

I am filled with curiosity. I am nervous and excited but also somewhat bewildered by the whole environment. Most of all, I have a sense of anticipation.

We tiptoe gingerly through cramped and darkened alleyways where women sit making dresses on treadle sewing machines while a few others work on machines powered by personal generators. We are flanked by rickety shops in various stages of disrepair, selling a wide variety of goods covered in dust.

As a foreigner, I am overwhelmed by the disorder and a vague sense of danger.

Finally, we arrive at the school, which is situated at the end of a long alley behind a light-blue picket fence. A sign made of lateral two-by-fours with lots of gaps and holes has also been painted in the same light blue. "Paulina's Queensland School" is emblazoned above the doorway. The entrance is past a rickety bridge covering a hole over which you must hop over to get into the first classroom. It is a nursery, a crèche with a dirt floor, and there are no toys. I was very taken aback and confused by this.

In Ghana, most schools provide lunch for the children, for which parents pay a small fee. At this one, there is an open-pit fire for cooking in the middle of an earthen floor. Little children are running about, and the teachers are watching them, but they don't seem to be controlling them. I feel an urgent need to shout, "Get the kids away from the fire!" but I know that would be terribly inappropriate. This is not my school. It is not my business to judge or even to offer solutions. I am here to observe, to listen, and to learn.

Paulina comes to greet us. She is dressed in a blue linen shirt. She is poised and self-assured. She is open and friendly. Though she is not highly educated, she is clearly highly intelligent. She is quiet, soft-spoken, yet commanding, and I notice a sparkle in her eyes behind which lies kindness and a keen sense of humor. She looks slightly puzzled by my interest in her school but still takes me on a tour.

The school reflects the market. The infrastructure is in disrepair. She tells me between 100 and 150 students are enrolled. The toilet for those students is a single pink bucket that Paulina herself hoses out after every use. The school has a two-story wooden structure, and the staircase to the second level has no banister. The children navigate it carefully, knowing that they could easily slip between the slats of the stairs if they are jostled or fooling around with one another while traversing the steps.

The classrooms are dark. A single lightbulb is rigged up in most rooms. Exposed wires droop down, hanging like snakes. The floorboards have huge gaps in them and look as if they will give way at any second.

Classroom sizes are surprisingly manageable, with twenty-two to twenty-six children in each. Paulina's son is well educated and teaches fourth grade, which he tells me is the highest level that the school serves so far. He is an excellent teacher—energetic and enthusiastic. He is animated and excited to teach. He engages the children beautifully, and they, in turn, are excited to learn.

I speak to the children. Since I grew up in Australia, I show them where Australia is on a map. I ask them to tell me what their dreams are. What do they want to be? I discover they have dreams of big careers. They tell me they want to be doctors, airline pilots, actors, and architects. Or engineers, accountants, teachers, and lawyers. One wants to be a physicist and work at NASA. They seem to be informed about the world around them. Given their circumstances, I am astounded that they are. Then I wonder whether any of them will be able to realize these dreams.

I sit down to speak with Paulina. The school has become her life's work and her driving passion. I tell her that I have seen a film about schools like hers and that I have come to Ghana with many questions.

"How do you finance your school?" I ask her. "Do you take loans?"

One of the tools that has been widely used to fight poverty is the microloan, a type of financing that provides small loans to entrepreneurs who would usually be denied access to capital because they are too poor.

"No," says Paulina. "I have been unable to access a loan for my school. I have a wholesale yam business, and I use some of the profits from that to run the school. I do take loans for my yam business. I have been a very creditworthy client for years, but when I ask for a loan to improve my school, I am declined. So, I rely on the profits from my yam farming and distribution business to make any school improvements."

I learn that the school brings in little to no profit, and despite the success of her yam business, she is far from becoming wealthy. She has nonetheless managed to create a working school, pay the teachers, and provide school uniforms, which she sews herself.

"Do you get any support from government agencies?" I ask.

"I try not to go near them because I don't know what they're going to do," she shares. "They could close my school because it doesn't meet all their regulations. And then where would all these children go?" She gestures around the space.

I learn that she sleeps in her school to make sure that nobody steals any of her supplies. She has a home and a husband, but she worries about the school's security as well as that of the children, some of whom she watches after hours while their parents work late into the night.

I sit with Paulina for a long time, asking question after question, riveted by her answers.

"Why are these children not in a free government school?" I ask her.

"In my opinion, the nearest government school is poorly managed, and it is too far away from the market for most children to walk," she explains. "Those who can walk there must cross a busy road where several children have been killed. There have also been numerous kidnappings in the area where children have been abducted and held for ransom."

She tells me that it was the urging of parents within the market that compelled her to start her school. Eager to learn, I bombard her with more questions.

"Tell me again why you can't get a loan for school improvements?"

"The bank is a regulated financial institution, and they view a school loan as too risky," she says with a flicker of resignation. "They say they won't take such a risk, although I have paid back every single loan for my yam business on time. They have never extended a loan for my school!"

"Do you have a bank account for your school?" I ask her.

"No," she tells me. She hides what little money she has on the premises.

She charges just over the equivalent of US$5 per term, and out of necessity, the school operates year-round without vacations. It becomes clear to me that the school has been established in response to very strong market demand.

I am overwhelmed by what I am learning. I am sick to my stomach. I am angry. Not at Paulina, of course, but at the circumstances in which she finds herself and the conditions in which her students are forced to learn. The facts are hard to digest. I walk out of the building and think, *This cannot be!*

In the coming years, I will learn that Paulina's school is representative of millions of others in developing economies.

What I didn't know at that moment was that this encounter, this meeting with Paulina, would change my life.

PART I

A PHILANTHROPIC AWAKENING

Chapter 1

HOW IT ALL BEGAN

One of the great motivators in my life has always been the frustration and anger I feel whenever I encounter inequity and injustice. Many people feel this way but all too often think they are not able to do anything about it.

I was born in Ireland, but my parents moved to London during World War II. They immigrated to Australia when I was four years old so that my mother, who had a lung condition, could live in a very dry climate. We lived in a pair of gold-mining towns just three miles apart from each other called Kalgoorlie and Boulder.

Each had one main street, many pubs, and a good number of brothels. This was a great culture shock for my mother, used to the sophistication of London and its bustling streets. My father had secured a job as the general director of the British-owned Kalgoorlie Power and Lighting Corporation that supplied power to the townships and gold mines. Most of the town's population worked in the mines or for the power station. We lived a decidedly middle-class existence in a company-owned house specially held for the general director. Many of my friends and classmates were less fortunate. They lived in handcrafted homes largely constructed of corrugated iron. Many children showed up for school barefoot, even in the dead of winter. I was largely unaffected by this disparity, and it wasn't until I started at the University of Western Australia, where I was a social anthropology and economics major, that my consciousness was raised, and I had my first adult encounters with systemic inequities.

Social anthropology is really social economics, so the two majors complement each other. My teachers were some of the world's most respected experts in many geographies, but most particularly Aboriginal Australia. I learned that every social group is fundamentally an economic group. I believe to this day that social economics and social anthropology should always be taught together.

As undergraduates, we could align ourselves with a doctoral student to do research for them, which mostly involved going to the library to find articles. Everything was card-cataloged at the library, and it took hours to get results. In exchange, we were invited to join the doctoral students on some remarkable excursions onto indigenous lands where we studied ancient cave paintings.

This is when I became aware of—and shocked by—what was being done to the indigenous peoples and the disdain with which white people treated them. They had been relocated from their traditional lands—their way of life completely erased. Most Australians made no real attempt to understand them. Indigenous Australians had a sophisticated culture that was centered in a very peaceful way of living. Although they had no written language, it was obvious from their elaborate kinship system, which had to be memorized, that they had a deeply complex civilization.

Over the course of these excursions and classes, I learned the dangers of colonialism and the damage that can be done when dominant cultures engage with nondominant cultures without truly understanding them, which inevitably results in exploitation. This lesson didn't end with my studies; it has shaped the way I see the world ever since.

After graduating from university, I taught school for a year and then decided to make a change. However, this short-lived experience was so impactful that it would stay with me all the way until I started the foundation. I had no idea then how relevant the experiences I had as a new teacher, feeling ill-prepared and scared in front of a classroom, would help me understand the challenges teachers are facing in all the schools I would go on to support later.

In 1972, I found myself working for Hyatt International in Sydney, Australia. It was there that I met my future husband and eventually moved to Chicago.

I didn't experience much of a culture shock moving from Australia to the American Midwest. The people in Chicago reminded me very much of the people in Sydney. However, there was a weather shock because I arrived at Thanksgiving, and it was freezing cold. Once I started a family, I filled my time by going to grad school at the University of Chicago, where I decided not to continue with anthropology but instead chose to broaden my education by studying English language and literature. One of my areas of study was the political rhetoric of eighteenth-century America, focusing on the significant debates between the English Parliament and colonists in America. My intention was to teach myself about my new home, and my studies provided me with a great understanding of American history. I got my master's in 1984, and much to my delight, I was invited to stay on for a doctorate. However, by that time I wanted to remain at home and concentrate on the great adventure of being a parent.

Unfortunately, my marriage did not last, but we had two wonderful children together, Matthew and Liesel. I thought I would eventually return to teaching, but once again, it seemed that the universe had other plans for me.

BEYOND WEALTH: A NEW PURPOSE UNFOLDS

In 2005, both Liesel and Matthew came into significant family wealth, and since I'd been managing my own investments for many years, they both asked me to manage their money until they felt confident in managing their own affairs.

When Liesel was twelve and Matthew was nearly fourteen, despite their young age and against everybody's advice, I started to take them to investment management meetings. In case something happened to me, I wanted my children to know how to invest their money, so I put structures in place so that they would have control over their own funds—and prayed to God that they would make smart decisions.

The gist of what I told them was, "There are a lot of real sharks out there, and they will look at your youth and inexperience and see you as easy targets and envision enormous profits for themselves. So, you must pay attention and learn what I am teaching you. Then others will see that you know what you're doing, that you know how to ask tough questions on your own, and that you understand the answers. That way, no one can take advantage of you."

Looking back, I see that at its core, this was about more than just financial literacy. It was about ensuring they had the resources and knowledge to protect and shape their own futures—something every child deserves but not every child has.

Soon enough, the children were ready to take control of their own affairs. I had great confidence in the teams that I had selected to support them and felt that I had taught the children well. Liesel was particularly grateful. But what happened next left me completely thunderstruck. Knowing me as well as she does, she knew

> Looking back, I see that at its core, this was about more than just financial literacy. It was about ensuring they had the resources and knowledge to protect and shape their own futures— something every child deserves but not every child has.

that the greatest gift she could ever give me was to provide significant funding for a foundation and ask me to run it and take ownership of it. As a matter of fact, she had already arranged to do it.

I was simultaneously stunned, overjoyed, and terrified. *Oh, my God!* The responsibility was enormous. As excited as I was, I had no idea how to run a foundation. I was clueless. It was like someone had just asked me to perform brain surgery.

Now, I had always been philanthropically inclined, but until that moment, most of my giving had been in support of medical research. I believe that Liesel assumed I would expand upon this interest, writing checks here and there, and that was certainly where my initial impulses leaned.

I had never really had any sense of structure in the way I donated, but I really wanted to live up to the trust Liesel had placed in me. I spent weeks thinking about the task ahead. I dug deep down inside myself to decide how I wanted the foundation to function. I knew that I would never be content to just be a check-writer, and I knew I wanted to tackle inequality. To do this well, I had to run the foundation in an impactful and sustainable way that wouldn't depend on renewing grants over and over.

But I just didn't know how—yet.

As it turned out, I was about to take a dramatically different turn in how I engaged with the world philanthropically.

From a legal perspective, the first thing we had to do was name the foundation. My treasurer decided on "The IDP Foundation," using the three initials of my name—Irene Dryburgh Pritzker. I expected to change the name later once we knew the focus of the foundation, but as it happened, we didn't need to. After my first trip to Ghana in 2008, I developed a vision for the foundation and went through the dictionary, reading every word that started with an I, D, or P. Eventually I settled on *Innovation*, *Development*, and *Progress*, and today nobody thinks of the foundation initials as standing for anything else. Innovation, development, and progress represent the approach of the IDP Foundation precisely, whether through grants or investments.

Around this time, because of my history of giving to medical research, I was invited to chair a big gala for the American Association for Cancer Research, on whose board I served. One of the main responsibilities of chairing any gala is to sell as many tables as you can to your friends and colleagues. However, there is usually an expectation of reciprocity when you do so, a quid pro quo, if you will. I invited my friend Stella Boyle to the gala. She was very involved with a group called Opportunity International (OI), of which I had never heard. Stella invited me to a presentation on the power of microfinance, which was OI's main business. I'd also never heard of microfinance before, so I didn't know what to expect.

The presentation was held in a historic home in downtown Chicago. I found it incredibly engaging and started to research microfinancing. The idea took hold in my mind since it is by its very nature sustainable, and it occurred to me that Liesel might be interested as well.

Soon after, I was invited to a fundraising dinner at Stella's house. Stella had a beautiful home on the lake, and the weather was just perfect—a lovely evening altogether. Many attendees were either already supporters or potential supporters. It was a typical fundraising event. Intrigued by microfinance, Liesel joined me.

At the event, we were shown a short film that explained the work of OI. Our interest had been piqued, and we were invited to California to participate in what they called the President's Forum, a fundraising conference with an impressive list of speakers. So out to Palm Springs we flew!

PALM SPRINGS 2008: IDPF FINDS ITS FOCUS

The conference venue was huge and decorated with beautiful large-scale pictures of African artisanal handicrafts along with some of the actual pieces, all made by recipients of microloans.

One of the keynote speeches was delivered by an English professor, James Tooley, who specializes in education in the developing world. He was not an armchair academic. He had made field trips for years all over the globe, getting into the weeds and seeing firsthand what conditions were like for some of the poorest people on earth. He gave a lecture and showed a short film that he had made in collaboration with the BBC for *Newsnight*.

The film is set in the slums of Lagos, Nigeria, specifically in Makoko, home to about fifty thousand people. It has been referred to as the "Venice of Africa," given that a third of the housing structures are built on waterways that stand in for streets, with rickety and run-down buildings held up by stilts. Canoes ferry residents between neighborhoods. Professor Tooley, in his narration, notes that Makoko is one of the poorest settlements on the African continent.

There are vibrant drums and the sound of children singing and playing in the background. Tooley tells us he believes there to be a secret here to be uncovered. And indeed, there is. As unlikely as it sounds, he has discovered several flourishing private schools. The camera cuts to children performing a concert of traditional drumming and singing. They are joyful, passionate, and brimming with enthusiasm. The scene transitions to a series of classrooms, tightly packed together and separated only by blackboards, where learning is unfolding with vibrant energy. He tells us that 70 percent of the children in Makoko are educated in these kinds of schools.

However, these private schools are not elite establishments for the wealthy. These are schools sustained by some of the poorest people on earth: at the time of filming, the average income for a family was around US$50 a month, and school fees were five or six dollars a month. He interviews a series of parents who feel that the free government public schools are a waste of their children's time. Professor Tooley then interviews the government official in charge of education for the area. She dismisses the parents as ignorant, the schools as dysfunctional, and the reason for their existence as simply that parents wish to be able to say they are sending their children to a private school, that their primary interest is in claiming a "fake status symbol."

However, this claim is belied by the footage that follows. The filmmakers visit a public school. The classroom is overcrowded. When, in the middle of a rote learning routine, a teacher takes a cellphone call, instruction grinds to a halt—it was a wrong number. Her students are bored and disaffected, and some are even sleeping. In the next classroom we visit, the teacher is fast asleep with his head down on his desk. *How can this be?* The commissioner of education is interviewed next, and he states that complaints about public schools may have had merit in the past, but everything has been fixed now. Clearly not.

We cut back to the private school where the physical condition is dire. There don't seem to be any learning materials. Even so, the teacher has a textbook and works from a dusty blackboard as he vibrantly and passionately shares knowledge with his engaged and fully alert students.

Tooley tells us that his team has randomly tested around three thousand students—and the private school attendees consistently outperform the public school students.

The film affected me deeply. When the screening was over, Tooley continued his address. This phenomenon, he told us, occurs throughout the developing world. The lecture concluded, and I sat there confounded, trying to process this information. I was quite literally speechless. But I was also fascinated and hungry to learn more.

After the lecture I approached an OI executive and asked, "Where did you find James Tooley? That was a very powerful presentation."

He responded, "You know, the reason James is here is because we are thinking of starting an 'edu-finance' program. We would like to create loan products specifically to lend to schools."

OI had been making microloans to entrepreneurs of all kinds in Ghana. One class of recipients happened to be schools, though schools had not been specifically targeted. After being shown

Professor Tooley's research, OI had contacted him and started thinking about ways to support education in developing countries like Ghana, particularly since so very many lower-income people were already sending their children to low-fee private schools for all the reasons elucidated in Tooley's film.

OI eventually asked me whether I would like to come to Ghana and see what they had planned and were thinking of developing.

"Yes!" I said at once, without a moment's hesitation. And Liesel joined in, saying, "I'll come, too!" And there we were, ready to go to Ghana.

OFF TO GHANA

As it happens, I had a very personal connection to Ghana. During World War II, my father worked as an electrical engineer for the British Foreign Office, mostly in hydroelectric plants (and indeed anything that generated electricity). Before and during the war, he had lived in Nigeria, Ghana, India, and Kenya. He may have been posted to so many challenging locations because of his great facility with language.

Out of all these countries, he had loved Ghana the most and frequently spoke of it. He spoke fluent Twi, a dialect of Akan spoken by Ghanaians in the central and southern regions. Was my father's experience some sort of sign? Was he watching over me and sending me there? The more time I spent in Ghana, the more I believed that this was the case. He had always believed in Ghana's potential and had maintained that if any country could lift the economic fortunes of Africa, it would be Ghana.

I was excited to go. I'd never been to any country in sub-Saharan Africa. On that first trip, we stepped off the plane into the scorching sun, hauling our rolling suitcases down the aircraft stairs and onto the tarmac. I was overwhelmed by the blistering heat and prayed there would be air conditioning in the hotel. The airport, jam-packed with people, was utter chaos. As we made our way out, we were greeted by a mass of people holding up a myriad of signs and taxi drivers looking for fares. We battled our way through the crowds and found our driver and the OI staff member, a young man named Andy Sprunger, who had been assigned to pick us up, and we headed to our hotel.

As we drove, I was fascinated by how vibrant the scene was outside the car window. The heavy traffic gave us time to take in our surroundings, the roads lined with merchants selling a random array of goods: three-piece sofa sets, garden gates, an assortment of brightly colored fabrics, shelving units, desks, shoes, and anything else you could possibly imagine. And the noise! People shouting, hawking their wares, competing for customers, and interacting with one another. Often, as they saw our white faces, people would shout out, "*Obroni, obroni, obroni,*" which historically and literally means "not to be trusted" but has in the postcolonial era become a neutral term in Ghana for white people.

We arrived at the hotel and were taken to our rooms. There was a market situated outside the hotel in the distance, and loudspeakers were blaring; the noise carried all the way to my room. It seemed as if all the people in the market were shouting at the top of their lungs.

I realized that up to this point, I had led a very sheltered life. Well, that was all about to change.

The trip turned out to be a sort of internal review and workshop for OI. The focus of the workshop was helping OI get better at measuring social outcomes that could be interpreted as a direct result of their programming. Liesel and I weren't quite sure how we fit into their process, but we participated.

In the meantime, in between these various meetings, OI arranged for us to see some of the schools that they hoped to bring into their edu-finance loan program. Much to my frustration, they were nothing like the schools we had seen in Professor Tooley's film. The schools we were taken to weren't glamorous. They weren't elite by any stretch of the imagination. But they all had permanent buildings, proper classrooms, and teaching and learning materials. These schools were not why I had traveled to Ghana.

I expressed my disappointment to the team at OI. The fundraising film they'd shown to donors led them to believe they would be making donations to address sustainable programming for some of the poorest schools in the world. In reality, it seemed OI was looking to support more established schools because they considered them more reliable loan subjects.

"What am I doing here?" I asked. "Have I come all this way for nothing?"

At this point, one of the OI loan officers saw my frustration and quietly pulled me aside and said, "Let me take you to some of the kinds of schools I think you want to see."

That was how I came to be in the Agbogbloshie Market. That is how I met Paulina Nlando and where my life truly changed. This was the area I wanted to research thoroughly, which might well become the primary focus of our foundation.

After my visit to Paulina's school, we found no less than eight schools within the same marketplace! All faced enormous challenges. One of them was located inside a ramshackle, poorly constructed church—a very long, thin, flimsy building with an earthen floor. The owner of the building, the church's minister, was charging exorbitant rent for use of the space. The classrooms were separated by blackboards on stands, which meant it was exceptionally noisy. The children, lacking desks, sat on the floor. *How on earth could anyone concentrate and learn in such conditions?*

I saw similar edifices—dark, dank, and run-down, with large rooms where children congregated around poorly resourced, untrained teachers, most of whom had finished high school but struggled to teach under such difficult conditions, as anyone would. Later I learned that all the teachers in the schools I visited followed the Ghana education curriculum as best they could. But unfortunately, the teachers emphasized rote learning, which was all they knew. There was a distressingly liberal use of the cane even on the littlest, youngest, and most vulnerable children.

The scene took me back to my own childhood in Australia. In my school, Boulder Primary, there were public canings. It was brutal. The sadistic deputy headmaster lined students up on Monday mornings, and they had to hold out their hands. The kids knew that they were going to be caned, so they had spent all week living in fear. I saw the fear, and we all felt it together. I will never forget it.

But the comparison stopped there. I was keenly aware of the privileges I enjoyed, even in Kalgoorlie. Many of my fellow pupils may not have had money to buy shoes, but we studied in solidly constructed, free public schools, were taught by trained teachers, and had ample resources.

I became a trained teacher myself at a time when there were very few trained teachers with university degrees in Australia. Most teachers attended two- or three-year programs at a teacher training college. Getting a teacher with a university degree was a fantastic opportunity for any school, so I was immediately placed teaching English and economics to high school seniors. It was terrifying.

All I had was a syllabus for each subject. It was up to me to create the curriculum and individual lesson plans—something I had never done before, despite being taught how in teacher training college. It was an incredibly challenging experience.

It wasn't the teaching itself that I minded. I loved it and was well qualified. The issue was that I was teaching students who hoped to matriculate. I took this responsibility deeply to heart. If I screwed up, they wouldn't matriculate. Consequently, I allowed my work to consume me. I felt as though I did not see sunshine for a full academic year, and I had little to no recreation time because I was always cooped up inside preparing for class. There was, of course, no Google or internet in those days, just libraries and card files. Furthermore, with no past lesson plans for referral, I had to design a year's worth of work by myself.

Back in the market, reflecting on the school where I had taught and the challenges I faced—even with a university degree and a teacher training certificate—I couldn't help but notice how much greater the difficulties were for the schools around me. The challenges they faced seemed impossible in comparison. *These kids have no chance*, I thought. These teachers aren't professionally trained and have no teaching and learning materials. The average child's performance is completely compromised. These schools, students, and teachers are powerless and marginalized by the rest of the world because they are poor. No one seems to care about them.

I was flabbergasted and angry to the point of being speechless. The sense of an inexorable reality consumed me as I finally truly understood that these were not isolated circumstances but the unavoidable consequences of the world in which these communities were forced to live. How unfair. If children aren't given a good education, then the odds against their having any kind of success in life become massively stacked against them. Yet, here they were—kids coming to these schools each day eternally filled with hope. These schools are exactly what I perceived to be low-fee private schools.

Just to be clear, I think it's important to define exactly what I mean by a low-fee private school.

As with Paulina's school, low-fee private schools are schools that have arisen to address a need in their communities. Usually, they are managed by their proprietors—entrepreneurs who are motivated to provide their poverty-stricken neighbors with an alternative to government schools. They often bridge a gap when there is no government school available or it's too far from where students live, and therefore these private low-fee schools should be seen as complementary to public education rather than competing with it. Neither school is free, but low-fee private schools on average cost as little as 25 percent more than the expense of sending a child to a government school, and as you will see, most parents are willing to strive to meet the extra expense and provide a better education for their children.

But why are low-fee private school numbers growing at an exponential rate in Ghana and across the developing world? There are many reasons, but let's focus on Ghana:

- There are many expenses associated with attending "free" government schools: bus fare, lunch fare, facilitation fees, exam fees, and enrollment fees, for instance.

- The class sizes in public schools can be enormous, with as many as eighty to one hundred children in a classroom. To accommodate the number of students, the schools sometimes are forced to schedule a morning shift and an afternoon shift for different groups of students. Under such circumstances, it is almost impossible to provide individualized attention to students, not to mention differentiated learning. Remember that Paulina's school has only twenty-two to twenty-six students per classroom—and she refuses to let the class grow beyond that size.

- Control over the schools is centralized in Accra and largely controlled by the teachers' union, effectively rendering head teachers in the field powerless to remove poorly performing teachers, even when they don't show up on a regular basis. Often, when a government-trained teacher doesn't like their posting, they just don't show up for work. We witnessed teachers asleep in their classrooms and heard that teachers have shown up drunk. We observed teachers congregating outside or inside classrooms, socializing and having a good time while their students ran amok. Rarely is anything ever done to punish such behavior. The teachers' unions are strong, which has its benefits, but the union invariably sides with the teacher, which makes remedying these situations difficult.

The parents we spoke with articulated their desire for better supervision of their children, better governance in the schools, smaller class sizes, and, in general, stricter regulations. They liked the fact that the proprietor of a private school could and would immediately fire a teacher who didn't show up for work without a very good excuse.

After seeing these schools, and particularly Paulina's school, I became more and more convinced that something needed to be done. Since OI was starting an edu-finance program, I brought one of their executives to see Paulina's school, and I asked him, "How many loans has she taken out for her yam business—and hasn't she repaid every single one on time? Why won't you give her a loan to improve what you can see is clearly dangerous infrastructure in dire need of repair?"

He responded simply. "These types of schools are too risky. She doesn't have the title to her land. She has no collateral. She has literally nothing that a bank would want should she default on a loan."

This is true for most of these low-fee private schools. No bank would want its infrastructure as collateral. The only thing they might be interested in is the land on which the school is built, if the proprietor has a clear title to it. It was hard to argue with the reality of the situation.

Paulina, for example, thought she owned a title to her land, but as it turned out, she didn't, even though she had a piece of paper that the person who "sold" her the land had given her. This was clearly not a legal document. And when I looked into how long it would take her to get a proper title, I was told it could take years.

On paper, Paulina is truly a high-risk loan client. However, on the basis of Paulina's track record in paying back her loans, is she really that much of a risk? I saw a loan to her as a potentially sustainable opportunity. But this would take some investigation. Researching this would require money. My opinion is that spending money in the form of grants to research a sustainable solution is the way that successful philanthropy *should* work.

So after an OI executive unequivocally told me that they could not make a loan under these circumstances, I was frustrated—angry—enough to blurt out, "Well, somebody ought to!"

He responded, "I'm looking forward to seeing how you're going to do it."

A challenge had been issued. And though I didn't know what to do next, I fully intended to figure out how to do it.

Chapter 2

FINDING A NICHE

Where to begin? And how to begin?

I asked myself a lot of questions. I asked everyone a lot of questions.

I knew I wanted to focus on marginalized, low-fee private schools. What I didn't know was how. I knew that these schools were complementary to the government-supported state schools. They were offering an alternative when the state was unable to fulfill its educational requirements.

When I got home from that first trip to Ghana, I made it my business to take advantage of whatever connections I had, which were not many at all. One of the first people I thought of was Elizabeth Littlefield, then CEO of the Consulting Group to Assist the Poor (CGAP)—a global partner of thirty-five development organizations working to help people in poverty through financial inclusion. CGAP is housed at the World Bank. Elizabeth delivered a speech at the Opportunity International (OI) conference in Palm Springs that elucidated some of the problems surrounding poverty globally. I reached out to her, and she was kind enough to agree to meet me in Washington, DC. I told her about the foundation and about the impact that James Tooley's speech and film had on me, but I also admitted that I had no experience in running a foundation.

When we talked about the film, I asked, "Who's helping these schools? If there are people contributing, who are they and what are they doing? Does the world even know about them?"

Elizabeth listened carefully to me and told me that she did not think any organization was actively addressing this particular sector. She also gave me invaluable advice on how to create an effective foundation: find a niche that resonates deeply with you, one that isn't being adequately addressed; conduct research as if you were preparing for a doctoral thesis; and make that the foundation's central focus.

"Well," I replied, "I think I found it with these low-fee private schools!"

So many questions came to mind: What about grants? Was there a willing patron? Was it going to be me? Maybe loans would be better. Could I design appropriate loan products? Who would partner with me? How was I going to pay for the discovery phase? And what exactly did I expect to discover?

THE SEARCH FOR A SUSTAINABLE SOLUTION

There was one thing I was certain of at that point: Any grant or loan I was going to make would never go directly to the financially unsophisticated school owners but would be managed by an objective intermediary.

My reasoning was this: If I gave grants directly to proprietors, no matter how large, there was little chance the funds would lead to sustainable growth for the school. Worse, they could easily be misused. Also, as soon as we, for whatever reason, stopped funding a school, it would be at risk of closing if the proprietor depended on the next donation rather than focusing on creating a *sustainable* source of income. Surviving on one grant after another, proprietors would not have the opportunity or incentive to develop any real understanding about how their schools could become stable and scalable.

So, I concentrated on planning to find out how proprietors were trying to solve problems themselves. Seeing for myself the challenges that all these thousands of mom-and-pop schools were facing, I might find the similarities, the strengths, weaknesses, obstacles, and threats they were facing (a SWOT analysis, as it's known). I would examine their best efforts at navigating these challenges and see whether I could develop my own skills and resources to help them progress in a sustainable way. I had to ask the right questions and listen carefully to the answers.

Unfortunately, these proprietors were not doing a good job of solving their challenges by themselves. They were merely subsisting hand to mouth, trying to keep their school doors—if they had any—open. Yet despite the challenges, 40 percent of all Ghanaian schools were low-fee private schools—and their numbers were growing by leaps and bounds.

I wanted to find out who else was working in this field and see if I could collaborate with them. This was the task my daughter had given me: to find a mission and give it all my energy. I wasn't going to just outsource the work. I had to figure it out on my own. It was a daunting task.

OI was starting to realize that, given its lack of ability to support the type of school that sparked my interest, I might need a different partner. Given my reaction in Accra, they knew that trying to keep me engaged in their edu-finance program was basically a lost cause.

On a subsequent trip to New York, I was invited to a dinner at which I was introduced through OI to Joseph Hewton, the chairman of the board at Sinapi Aba Trust (SAT). OI thought that I might be more successful working with SAT, which is a nonprofit microfinance trust. They have branches in all regions of Ghana, and they reach rural areas. As a trust, they have more leeway than savings and loan banks, which are regulated by the Central Bank.

As stated on their website, SAT is a non-governmental organization (NGO) that "provides microfinance services to entrepreneurs in small and microenterprises in Ghana with the objective of improving their business and enhancing income-generation opportunities of the low-income people to alleviate poverty, improve their standard of living, and consequently positively transform their lives."* SAT was well known to OI, and although SAT is neither owned nor operated by them, it is a member of the OI Network. SAT is headquartered in Kumasi, about 270 kilometers north of Accra.

Joseph said he'd be delighted to work with me and invited me to see him in Kumasi. I agreed to visit with him and the CEO of Sinapi Aba—a gentleman named Tony Fosu—the next time I was in Ghana.

Our conversation pulled me back to my visit with Paulina. Her story had left a lasting impact on me. Often, I ruminate over things

---

* Theophilus Tei Ayanou et al., "An Impact Assessment of Microfinance Institutions on Women Entrepreneurs in Small and Medium Enterprises: A Case Study of Sinapi Aba Trust," Kwame Nkrumah University of Science and Technology, Department of Accounting and Finance, May 2011, https://www.academia.edu/7632817/.

that I feel are unjust or that unjustly affect the lives of the people I care about, and I had come to deeply care about her and all those little children I had met. So, I planned a return visit to Ghana to see how SAT and my foundation might invent something that could de-risk individual loans to single-school owners.

Upon return to Ghana, I had breakfast with the new head of the Opportunity International Savings and Loans (OISL) program. I expressed my interest in working with SAT. He was not pleased, viewing SAT as direct competition, and he was angry that I would be disloyal to OI. I was quite bewildered. OI had connected me with SAT. Why was I now experiencing pushback from this person?

The reason we had such a combative meeting never became clear, but in the end, it all worked for the best. I abruptly left the meeting, got a car, and headed straight for Kumasi, a six-hour drive, to meet with Sinapi Aba. That visit resulted in a relationship that would shape the first and most important focus of the foundation and would consume my life to this day.

THE (MUSTARD) SEEDS OF CHANGE

SAT was founded in 1994 by a group of Christian leaders in Ghana who wanted to create a foundation to help lift some of the country's most vulnerable citizens out of poverty. The initial vision for the foundation was conceived by Bishop Davis John Freeman, who is credited as the trust's vision bearer. Reverend Kwabena Darko, one of Ghana's most successful entrepreneurs, was the first chairman of the board. Darko had been loaned money to start a poultry farm in 1966. His farm became enormously successful, and he never forgot the importance of his first small-business loan. He worked with the founding members to create a structure for the foundation.

> The trust's mission is "to serve as a mustard seed through which opportunities for enterprise development and income generation are provided to the economically disadvantaged to transform their lives."

Sinapi Aba means *mustard tree.* Mustard seeds, which are very tiny, grow into very large trees. The trust's mission is "to serve as a mustard seed through which opportunities for enterprise development and income generation are provided to the economically disadvantaged to transform their lives." Since SAT's inception, it has given hundreds of thousands of loans to small businesses throughout Ghana, mostly through a trust group mechanism, where members of a trust group assume responsibility for all members to repay their loans on time. We did not see the trust group mechanism to be viable for school lending, so our plan was to design products for individual loans. This would be a first for SAT.

Tony explained to me that he had always wanted to lend to very poor schools, but his credit committee would not allow him to engage in such a risky venture. I suggested that we develop a loan program with a US$1.5 million grant. OI offered to be the delivery conduit and seemed keen to keep our relationship active. A US$1.5 million grant would remove all financial risks to SAT. Two-thirds of the grant would be used to fund the costs of developing the program, and the remaining US$500,000 would be used to experiment with a loan portfolio and the rest. Tony thought for a minute when he heard this and then broke into a big smile. "What you are saying is music to my ears," he said. "I very much want to find a way to provide capital to these schools. Yes, we can. We are interested. We will start to model a loan program and try to have it ready for your next visit."

I returned to Chicago. Creating a loan program was not going to be an easy task. We needed much more information to get started. We needed to know the cash flow of these schools and how big they were on average. How do they differ from one another?

For example, the cash flow of a school in a cocoa-growing region would differ significantly from that of Paulina's school in the Agbogbloshie Market due to the way farmers are paid and the timing of tuition payments. Are school proprietors paid daily, or in rural areas, are they only compensated during harvest time? How could we structure the right financial product with an appropriate grace period? It was crucial to take the time to build a product that was tailored to these specific needs.

Since OI had made it clear that they would not support making loans to the kind of schools I wanted to support, this put our partnership in a very awkward position. But I was reluctant to sever ties with them completely and work with SAT only. To be honest, I felt as if I was being pushed out of the nest—OI wanted my support but wasn't interested in creating a new program for me. For that moment, I was stuck and didn't know how to proceed.

BURYING THE PARACHUTE

One night, Liesel and I were sitting in my living room, and I was spiraling. My hands were clenched in my lap, and I could feel the weight of the frustration building. I turned to her, my voice shaky. "I don't know how to do this if Opportunity International isn't able to come to the party."

Without missing a beat, Liesel met my gaze, her expression fierce. "You don't need Opportunity International!"

I blinked, stunned. "What?"

"You can do it yourself."

I paused, trying to make sense of her words. "What do you mean, I can do it myself?" I was starting to feel the heat rise in my chest. "You know I've already been to all these development agencies, and nobody can help me. It feels as though nobody is listening."

Liesel's voice didn't waver. She was resolute. "Just do it on your own!"

My frustration flared into anger. I shot back, my words sharp, "I would be in a country I don't yet understand, and without Opportunity International, who is going to help me?"

I stood up, pacing now, the tension in my body palpable. "How does the Ghanaian school system work? How do I meet with the right government officials? I don't have anybody to help me! What the hell do you expect me to do? Parachute out of an airplane in the middle of Ghana? Then what?"

She watched me, calm and unwavering, her eyes never leaving mine. Finally, her voice was low but steady.

"Bury the parachute. Get up. Walk until you find the nearest school. Start asking questions. Then listen. Then find more schools. Listen more."

I felt as though she was throwing down the gauntlet. I don't mind challenges—they can be very stimulating—but that kind of challenge from a daughter is in a whole category of its own.

The next day, I told her that I had decided it would be too hard to succeed without OI.

She responded, "If it was easy, somebody would've already done it. And you can do it! Think of all the things you have done in your life that have been hard, the challenges you have overcome."

She left me with a simple but powerful thought: "Mama, you'll figure it out. The first thing is: Be a joiner. Join every single organization related to the kind of program you want to run. And when you go to conferences or panels, introduce yourself to everyone you meet. Keep asking, keep asking, keep asking, keep asking. Who lends to these kinds of schools? What have they done that has been successful? What have they done that hasn't worked?"

She paused, her gaze steady. "You'll make your rounds. You'll see."

This was a challenge that I was sure was beyond me, no matter how passionate and indignant I felt about it. The possibility of not partnering with OI made me feel deeply insecure. Going it alone without their staffing infrastructure and experience in microfinancing would be an enormous responsibility. As far as I could tell, no one else was working with the kind of schools I wanted to engage in quite the way I wanted. I would be starting from scratch, inventing the wheel. It was terrifying. I had no experience in this arena and no confidence that I could succeed.

I started worrying like crazy. I couldn't sleep at night. I was a nervous wreck! I was torn between my fear of starting a whole new venture in Ghana—one I would essentially have to invent from scratch—and my deep concern about all the children who were just never going to have a real shot at getting a good education unless someone stepped in to help them. These children had no resources at hand to escape their environment. They were extremely poor children in extremely unresourced environments who had little chance of improving their lives. They were being robbed of any choice and any hope.

As I tossed and turned, I kept hearing Liesel's voice in my head.

When Liesel funded and cofounded the foundation, she said to me, "*You'll do something truly amazing. I just know you will.*"

In fairness, Liesel had initially thought that I would probably end up funding medical research because it had been a passion of mine for most of my life. This is what I thought as well, until I heard James Tooley speak, though medical research has also been a major focus of the foundation.

Eventually I realized that Liesel was right—I didn't need OI. But I still believed that the only way things were going to truly progress would be if I were to find a partner with whom I could initiate the program, and so I started to think more about SAT as the partner I needed, one that could provide the experience and expertise that I lacked.

If SAT and my foundation could create a program with a high level of loan repayment, there would be a positive financial return on investment for the financial institution through loan interest as well as social credit for SAT. A successful model might even encourage financial institutions in other countries to copy it once it had opened a new, reliable, and significant market.

These schools need loans. Schools are businesses. They are social enterprises. Even though the parents who send their children to these schools are desperately poor—often living on less than a dollar a day—circumstances force them to see education not as the universal right so often proclaimed, but as a commodity for which they must pay. They see these low-fee schools as the best choice for their children. For these schools to improve, they clearly need business loans.

But how could we give a business loan to a school that had no collateral? Who would be willing to take such a risk? This is where the philanthropist in me came to the fore. I was prepared to take the risk. I was ready to fund this experiment.

It was time to get to work—with SAT as my partner.

To create a successful pilot program, I first needed to evaluate the schools. Sitting at my desk in my Chicago office, over the course of a few hours, I came up with sixty-five questions that I wanted to ask low-fee private school proprietors so I could develop a program that would directly address the needs of their schools. The questionnaire was divided into two sections, one that addressed the general conditions of the school and the other addressing the way in which they financed their school. For excerpts from the questionnaire, refer to Appendix C.

My instincts told me that it was crucial that the program be crafted in collaboration with Ghanaians to answer the specific needs of Ghanaians. Imposing our own values and ideas onto the proprietors would most likely not work.

Taking inspiration from the image of a phoenix rising from the ashes, SAT and I decided to name the program the Rising Schools Program. And we prayed that our phoenix would have wings.

Chapter 3

THE PROPRIETORS

In any country, the only providers of education, teaching, and learning materials are either parents, funders, or governments. In the case of very low-fee private schools, the parents are too poor, the school owners can't afford trained teachers or to buy supplies, and the international development funders and governments won't include them in their planning.

How, then, could we hope that every child could have an equal shot at getting a solid education if we didn't address this gap? The problem, at this point, appeared to be unsolvable. But we had to start somewhere. And in my mind, there was no way we could achieve the goal of inclusion for all children without government support for trained teachers and teaching and learning materials.

So, on my next trip to Ghana, I set up meetings with some government officials to tell them what we were thinking of doing—despite many Westerners telling me, "Don't meet with the government. They will just serve to block and obstruct you."

I decided to find out for myself.

CHALLENGING ASSUMPTIONS, FINDING ALLIES

The Ministry of Education and the Ghana Education Service (GES) were my first ports of call. I felt certain that the government would not be my enemy. Surely, they cared just as much as I did about the children their services were unable to reach.

I reached out to Stephen Adu, the director of basic education, who held considerable authority in GES. He graciously agreed to meet with me. The offices at GES were quite run-down, with stacks of books everywhere that looked as though they hadn't been touched in years and rooms filled with old computers.

Stephen was a quiet, soft-spoken man with a commanding yet comfortable and amiable presence. I started by telling him about my experience at Paulina's school and how much I wanted to help.

"Oh, I know there are thousands of such schools, and we are not happy about them," he responded.

"Tell me why," I requested.

He was very matter-of-fact. "The number of these private schools keeps increasing," he explained. "Every day, more and more of them are opening. We don't know where they are. We don't know who's in them. We don't know what the teachers are like." He paused. "What we do know is that the students in these schools actually perform better than the students in public schools, but we don't know why, and it's very frustrating."

He continued, saying, "By the way, the word 'private' creates a great deal of controversy. You should know that there is significant political opposition to these schools from civil society and from the very powerful teachers' union."

"Why?" I asked.

"The teachers' unions object to the schools working with non-union labor. There are also a lot of misconceptions about the schools. There is a great feeling that these proprietors are simply profiteering off the very poor. *Profiteering!* That's the very word that is used by people who oppose private education."

"Well, that's ridiculous!" I said. "Paulina certainly isn't profiteering off anyone. She's barely subsisting." I told him about my intention to set up a program to provide microloans to schools like hers so that they could improve their infrastructure.

He was warming up to me, taking me more seriously as the conversation progressed.

"I am so pleased that you have come to speak with me first before setting up any program," he told me. "My colleagues and I, to be frank, are quite tired of dealing with well-meaning philanthropists who bypass the government. They waste enormous amounts of my time on ventures such as building schools without telling anyone. Once they've finished building them, they think that the schools will just run themselves—but without the necessary resources or support, that's simply not possible. Usually, the projects have been completed with donated money. So, when the donations dry up, the schools fall apart. And suddenly we're left to clean up the mess. You won't believe how many times I've been lectured by Western philanthropists on how we should fix the various problems we face. We know what our problems are!" he said.

"They are Ghanaian problems," he said, "not Western problems. You know, it would be nice if the Ghana Education Service, which manages the administration of all these schools, had more input into how these projects should be managed. Let me know how I can be of help."

"Honestly, I'm not sure yet," I told him. "I'm really just at the beginning of this journey."

"You seem to be interested at the moment in the primary level, yes?" he asked.

Up to that point, I'd mostly visited primary schools. I had no idea whether these low-fee private schools stretched into junior-high age. But it seemed that there was no way that the kind of schools I'd seen could encompass the needs of a high school education. Where would they get the equipment for a science lab, for instance? These kids didn't have access to computers. I told him that I'd seen teachers trying to teach IT by drawing a computer and a mouse on the blackboard to show their students what they look like.

"Yes, this is true," he said, shaking his head sadly. "These schools have no educational standards, and they are not even remotely regulated."

"I think if we can provide them with some capital, then we can help bring them up to regulation. Do you think this is feasible?" I asked.

He seemed pleased with the direction of the conversation. But he paused for a moment before saying, "Possibly. Yes. I do think you can make a difference. But don't forget, they have little in the way of teaching materials, and we don't know if they try to follow any standardized Ghanaian Education Services curricula."

I thought for a moment.

"You said you had standardized testing, yes?" I asked.

He said that there were Primary 2 and Primary 4 standardized tests. I explained that I wanted to evaluate the quality of the schools to be able to assess their educational needs. Their infrastructure needs were painfully apparent.

"Who administers those?" I asked.

"Well, that comes under the province of John Buckle," he said, reaching for his phone and dialing a number. "John, I'm sending someone over to meet with you."

Before I left, he stopped me and said, "You do know that things move quite slowly in Ghana."

I laughed and responded, "Well, if today's any indication, we're moving along quite rapidly, thank you." He chuckled, and off I went.

TRACKING EDUCATION

John Buckle worked with GES in the assessment and tracking of School Evaluation Assessment/National Evaluation Assessment (SEA/NEA) exams. He told me that he'd be happy to share the tests with me. The SEA test results were intended for curriculum development for school-level use in math and English (i.e., to determine what needs to be taught in greater depth). The NEA exam results were intended for national information and educational quality and policy evaluation—also in math and English. He was true to his word and sent the tests to me immediately.

After our meeting, John sent me over to the census department to meet Thomas Coleman, the coordinator for Education Monitoring Information Systems (EMIS) with the Ministry of Education. Thomas was responsible for figuring out how many children of school age were enrolled in school and what kind of schools they were enrolled in. This was an almost impossible task, even though private schools were required to be registered with the government as schools and as businesses.

"Most school proprietors won't register, though," he told me. "They are afraid we're going to shut them down."

"Here's a list of the names of all the schools that I know of in Ghana that are low-fee schools," he shared. "If you're going to do some investigating to find out the state of these schools, take this list with you as you go around. See if any of them match. And if any of them don't, write them in for me. And note the enrollment and the age group. Give it back to me so I know where they are."

"You're not playing tricks on me, are you?" I questioned. "You're not going to close these schools after I provide this information, right?"

He peered over his glasses at me and assured me, "That's not my department. My department is the census, and, of course, we know these schools exist. We just want to know where they are located. Where are these children going to school? Are they going to school? And what's happening in the school? So, of course, we want these schools to be registered with the government so that district officers can offer advice and attempt to regulate them."

"It would break my heart if I thought that I had come over here and caused the closure of many schools," I reflected. "It would be a terrible thing to do to these proprietors and the families of the children they are trying to serve." He told me he understood.

Over the course of these visits with the GES, I picked up some fascinating information. The right of private schools to exist is enshrined and protected in the Ghanaian constitution. However, most of these schools are unable to fulfill the requirements and regulations set out for them. If they could comply, they would be entitled to receive free in-service teacher training, textbooks, and school supplies. I pondered this information.

Perhaps my program could help get the schools up to code. Then they would be in great shape.

So, it was time to begin the adventure of touring Ghana to find as many schools as possible and ask the questions that I'd formulated in my Chicago office. We decided that we wanted to focus on schools that were either unregistered or low-rated by the government.

In Ghana, schools used to be classified as either A, B, C, or D schools. Every district had its own A, B, C, D, and Unregistered rating system. Unregistered was pretty standard for most of the schools, but if they did register, a district officer would come out and rate the following:

- The school, grading its infrastructure (whether or not they had actual classrooms and how safe they were, for instance)
- Availability of teaching and learning materials
- Teacher quality
- Ventilation quality and adequacy
- Water tank access
- Restroom access and sanitation

The scale was largely subjective and depended on the opinion of the GES team. It was also a sliding scale dependent on location. If the school was in Accra, in order to get an A, the bar was much higher than elsewhere because the resources in the capital are much better than in rural regions. A D school in Accra might very well be rated a B school if it were in a rural location.

ON THE ROAD

There were several of us working on the project now: six main players, including Tony Fosu, CEO of Sinapi Aba; Vincent Amponsah, also from Sinapi Aba; Liesel; Andy Sprunger; our amazing driver, Charles Adjei-Boateng; and me. Tony assigned his employee Kwaku Acheampong to be our point of contact and also introduced a bright, young addition to the team, Raphael Akomeah, who, prior to being brought into Sinapi Aba, had been a student at the university that Tony had attended.

In addition, Sinapi Aba was good enough to lend us cars from their carpool until I decided to purchase and send them two rugged Toyota SUVs from the United States. Sinapi Aba had advised us that they would be more reliable than cars made in South Africa; indeed, they were. They lasted twelve-plus years.

Although we were all chomping at the bit to create the program, we really couldn't begin designing it until we had completed and compiled enough fieldwork. The first thing we had to do was find the schools. It was often a challenge, as many didn't have proper buildings. But we climbed into our vehicles and began our search. Such was his passion and commitment to the project that Tony himself took the wheel. For a CEO with a heavy schedule to dedicate so much time to a project that ultimately represented quite a small percentage of the trust's portfolio was a remarkable gesture. I was both deeply moved by his engagement and even more energized to get things moving. Once we added the SUVs I had purchased, Tony and Charles shared the driving responsibilities.

Sometimes we would stop someone walking along the side of the road selling water, which they kept in a large container balanced on their head, and we'd ask, "Is there a school nearby?" Often,

they'd respond, "Just down there." We would begin trudging dutifully in the direction we'd been guided and, after about an hour,
realize that "just down there" could in fact mean ten kilometers!
We learned our lesson, and Charles took to asking, usually in Twi,
exactly how far "just down there" actually was!

Once we found the school, we would begin by introducing
ourselves to the proprietor and asking if they would be interested
in accessing a business loan. If they said yes, I would ask, "Would
you mind if we asked you some questions?" They'd often get a little
nervous, but then a member of our team would explain very clearly
in their local dialect what we were trying to do and that we understood what they were up against and wanted to help them.

In all, we interviewed around thirty school proprietors. My
original sixty-five questions were eventually expanded to more than
ninety, with the financial team adding a more sophisticated perspective. However, as we traveled through the country, we began to
pare the number of questions down, as we found we were taking
too much of the proprietors' time. They had schools to run, after
all.

The conditions of the schools varied. Some of them had buildings; some were simple canopies in the middle of a field. The ones
that had structured buildings often were run-down. They may have
been painted nicely some time ago, but now the paint was chipping
off. Windows were glassless—they were just open rectangles in the
wall to provide some ventilation. Some had finished floors, but most
had earth floors. Some had solid roofs, and some had roofs com-
posed mainly of straw, which meant that when it rained, the straw
mixture became moldy and rotten. Some had divisions between the
classrooms, but without doors, the classrooms were terribly noisy,

making it hard for children to focus. Some schools had classrooms that were simply trees in a field with blackboards nailed to them. Usually, when I asked if I could see learning materials, I'd be shown books that were grade inappropriate—the teacher was compelled to try and extrapolate from them what they thought the kids were capable of learning. The teachers were largely untrained. The proprietor usually had some sort of office, but the doors never had locks. In fact, there was no security of any kind to keep resources safe. Most schools had no toilet enclosures.

Although rural schools were generally rudimentary, one in particular became my favorite. It was situated in a huge field of grass outside a small village, far from any major city or town. It was basically a series of canopies that each marked the classroom areas. These "classrooms" were spread throughout the field. Each was separated from the others by a healthy distance, which meant that there were no distracting noises to compete with. Why did I fall in love with this school? It was in a truly beautiful green field, in the open air, surrounded by nearby trees, with lots of golden sunshine. I thought that if I were a child and had to pick one of these schools to be taught in, it would be here, surrounded by the glory of nature. But, of course, it too was unsustainable. When it rained, there was no school. And again, there were no toilets, just open pits out in the bush. But we stayed there for quite some time, playing with the children. We had plastic fifteen-ounce water bottles with us and thought nothing of them, but when we were finished with them, the children asked if they might have them—and subsequently had fun for hours making up games to play with them.

At that same school, I remember the delight the children took in looking at our digital camera images. For them, it was almost like magic to see themselves instantly captured on a tiny screen. Their joy was moving, memorable, and humbling.

Once we visited a nursery and kindergarten school outside of Kumasi run by an older woman and her daughter. We engaged in our usual process, asking all our questions, talking to the proprietor, and meeting her daughter.

We toured the school as usual and started by entering the nursery school section. There were rather a lot of children in the class, around forty, I think, and they were all around two-and-a-half or three years old. Anne Schumacher, whom I had hired as an executive assistant, had long, straight, platinum-blond hair. Most of the children, if not all, had never seen a white person, much less one with hair like that. Suddenly, a little girl at the very back of the room started to cry, which started a chain reaction. Pretty soon there were forty crying children in the classroom. At first, we were confused, then we realized that Anne was the cause. The children were terrified. They wondered whether they might be seeing a ghost or witch. The teacher tried to explain, saying, "These are *obronis* ["white person" or "foreigner"]. They've come to say hello, and they're our visitors." But it was useless trying to reason with children at this age. Anne hastily backed out of the room, but the howling continued.

At one of the classes for higher grades, we noticed a little girl standing outside the classroom looking in and watching the class. The building was just a long concrete wall with holes in it for the doors and the windows. I asked the proprietor, "Why is she standing looking through the window?"

The proprietor responded, "Her mother's a drunk and spends all her money on alcohol. She can't afford to pay for her education, and we can't afford any more scholarship children. But we feel really sorry for her, so we let her go to school by looking through the window."

Watching this child, standing all alone, so still for such a very long time, staring in through the window, haunted me. Although she was on the outside, she was yearning to be inside. She might as well have been in prison. I will never forget the image.

Everybody on our team emptied their pockets immediately, and we raised enough money to pay her school fees for the coming years. We gave the money directly to the proprietor, and before we left, a teacher arrived and led the little girl into the classroom.

She was no longer watching from the outside.

As we were wrapping up, the proprietor told us that she had recently had a heart attack. When she went into the hospital, she discovered that the doctor who was taking care of her had attended her nursery school. So, her school had given him a crucial start to continue with his studies.

LISTENING TO LEAD:
UNDERSTANDING PROPRIETORS' NEEDS

The proprietors of every school we visited shared much in common. They were always present at their schools. If they were ever away, it was on school business, and they invariably came back within fifteen minutes. Without fail, their prime motivation was to raise the level of education in Ghana and improve learning outcomes for their children. They wanted them to have a better life. They wanted to give them opportunities and hope, which would help them to build a better future for Ghana. They all recognized that a more educated country would be a more successful country. They were fueled primarily by hope and optimism, and just like Paulina, they believed that every child had the potential to grow up and be a huge success if only they had the experience of a good education. I saw very little despondency and despair.

I kept putting myself in the proprietor's shoes to understand their needs, desires, and visions. And I listened. I listened more than I've ever listened in my life. Sometimes our conversations would delightfully drift in all kinds of wonderful directions that had nothing to do with our project. They would tell me about their home lives and their own children, or they would ask me questions about my life and my children. Through these conversations, I gained more than just an understanding of the challenges these schools faced—I got to know the people behind them. The proprietors weren't just educators; they were dreamers, problem-solvers, and community builders. They had hopes, fears, and ambitions, just like everyone else. Just like you. Just like me. And yet, they were working with so few resources, making every step forward a challenge. In getting to know them, I also gained a deeper understanding of Ghanaian culture—its resilience, its generosity, and the shared human experiences that connect us all, no matter where we come from.

Each morning, a small amount of money was placed in their hand by parents as they dropped their children off. After paying their teachers and covering school expenses, there was usually little left for themselves—just enough to buy food and clothes and maintain their homes. I can safely say that none of them were profiteering.

Their financial literacy was limited. Most were just surviving from day to day. Often, they kept what little money they made in shoeboxes under their beds. Very few had bank accounts, and there was little understanding of the need to keep personal and business financial dealings separate.

Many of the parents were illiterate, but they were far from being stupid—and they didn't want their children to be illiterate. When I asked, "Why is it so important to you that you put your child in a private school?" the most common response I received was: "I have little faith in the public schools, and I want my child, my boy"—it was usually "my boy"—"to wear a suit and a tie. I want him to have that kind of job."

I kept my promise to Thomas Coleman at GES. I wanted to stay in the government's good graces. As we traveled, we used a satellite GPS marker we had picked up from an organization called Esri that provided us with the device at a generous discount. Wherever we found a school, we dropped a digital pin, and I would send the government an email. "These are the schools that we have discovered," I would tell them. "This is the general area that they are in. This is the name of the school. This is the proprietor. These are the qualifications of the owner of the school, and this is how many children they have enrolled: how many boys they have and how many girls." True to Thomas's promise, none of the schools were shut down.

Meanwhile, as we looked at our compiled survey results, we confirmed what we had long since suspected. The proprietors' answers were all similar. They needed textbooks and teaching and learning materials; they wanted better-trained teachers; most importantly, they would like access to capital so that they could put down a concrete floor or a roof or divisions between the classrooms.

Another thing we learned was that a good number of these schools were started by former public school teachers. They had retired and moved back to the village where they grew up, where they quickly realized there was a market demand for an affordable private school. Though these teachers were smart and had good entrepreneurial instincts, they were usually not equipped to run a business. Teaching a subject in a classroom is a very different proposition from managing an entire school. There was never a moment when they sat down and asked, "What is my business plan for this school?" The schools were growing organically but often without a sound business infrastructure.

Most of the proprietors had never dreamed that they would be able to get a business loan.

We believed that if a course in financial literacy and school management training was delivered to these school owners, it would be more likely that they could successfully carry out a loan to repayment. We argued that the model could be self-sustaining because we would factor the cost of the training into the loan terms.

We also began to assess the amounts of the loans, and we started to investigate building costs. While researching, we discovered that there was a lot of modular housing available made from used storage containers. They were quite durable and could withstand tropical conditions. However, to our surprise, upon showing this option to some of the proprietors, the idea was soundly rejected.

"I want a more permanent-looking structure," one of the proprietors told us. "It is very important to the parents that our school should appear stable. If they are going to pay money to send their children to school, it should be to a school made of concrete, not of temporary-looking, recycled storage units."

This was important feedback. It was vital that we listen to them and deliver what they needed. They knew their market better than

> "Nobody's ever listened to us before," they told us. "You make us feel as if we are somebody."

we did. And they, in turn, were surprised to be asked.

Designing a program without prior assumptions became the backbone of our work. We adopted a localized approach, which has now become a buzzword for development strategists, many of whom admit that they still don't have it right. One of the most striking experiences for me—and a frequent one—was how amazed the proprietors were when we asked what they needed. They were incredibly moved.

"Nobody's ever listened to us before," they told us. "You make us feel as if we are somebody."

Throughout this period, we continued to engage in numerous meetings with government officials, advocating on behalf of the proprietors. "If you close a school because they are not up to regulation," we declared, "where are these primary-aged children going to go to school? See this school? Look at this picture of it! Do you see it? Look at the condition it's in! Do you know how far away the nearest public school is? And this is the dangerous road these children would have to cross to get to that school—and some have already been killed! Let's work together, but please don't randomly close a school!" Clearly, they listened.

A BLUEPRINT FOR GROWTH:
TRAINING, LOANS, AND SUSTAINABILITY

Now that we had a very clear sense of what the schools needed, we started to work on the training modules for the proprietors. Our focus was on basic business and administrative principles that would help them sustain and grow their schools for long-term success. We had to establish the curriculum. We had to figure out how we were going to administer the program, and we needed to decide how the modules would be taught and by whom. We decided that we needed two teachers working in tandem at every training session and that we wanted to be consistent in what we were teaching. It was important to avoid having different proprietors learning different things at different times.

Once it was time to get to work creating the actual training manuals that would encompass the entire curriculum, we decided to create one version for the trainers and another for the proprietors.

Senior members of the Sinapi Aba staff, led by Tony and Vincent, met with Liesel, Andy, and me in Kumasi. We sat in the boardroom at Sinapi Aba's head office, combing through the surveys and working out what the proprietors knew and what they didn't know so that we could best position them for success. And we had no intention of wasting their time teaching them things they already knew.

We had hours and hours of brainstorming—with vibrant and lively discussions—as we drafted the essential areas that we thought would be most beneficial to cover in the training. Within a few weeks, a curriculum started to take shape.

We included sessions taken from Sinapi Aba's general client training manual. To those, we added sessions on the following topics:

- Costs and income
- Making a profit
- Separating personal and school finances
- Keeping good records

- Cash flow
- Ways to generate separate income
- Managing the loan itself
- The importance of having savings and cash reserves
- Teacher training and standards
- How to collect fees
- How to engage successfully with the Ghana Education Service
- Time management
- How to manage balance sheets
- How to create a business plan
- The importance of maintaining a school library
- Managing a good school lunch program
- Marketing the school
- Computers
- Crisis management
- How to keep teachers motivated

It was a huge amount of information, all of it essential. At the same time, we had to design the loan packages themselves. Sinapi Aba had a product they were already using for schools that needed to be refined and shaped to fit the purposes of our program. Although the entire team at Sinapi Aba was engaged in the process, we realized that to achieve a sustainable program, we needed outside help. We were lucky enough to have the services of Ken Koskela, a truly brilliant man who was working for Opportunity International (OI).

In his early days at OI, he created a financial model that was initially used for securing grants. OI had realized his work on the grant could be used by all the microfinance institutions for the purpose of planning. Subsequently it became a part of the OI business planning model, and then it continued to evolve. For our purposes, he took that framework and modified it, merging it with the Sinapi product to accommodate the fact that the IDP Foundation model was about more than just providing loans.

We went through multiple iterations of the budgets and loan packages, trying to work out how much subsidy might be necessary and over what period for the model to be sustainable.

Ken started by considering the inflation rate, which at the time was quite high—18 percent.

Ken started with three products. He began with infrastructure loans, then transportation loans for acquiring school buses, and then he modeled a loan for working capital for smaller, shorter-term loans, which could be used to address cash-flow issues. Proprietors have expenses throughout the year, but their revenues may only come in at a few points in time. A loan would aid in keeping the school running during those cash-poor times, like agricultural loans.

Around this time, Andy Sprunger, who had greeted Liesel and me when we first arrived in Ghana and proved himself invaluable after joining us full-time from OI, decided to move on to graduate school. We worked with OI to replace him and were lucky enough to bring Anne Hainer on board. Anne had just finished a graduate degree in social policy with a focus on health and education at American University in DC, so she was eminently qualified. She moved to Kumasi in early September 2009 and got to work right away, taking the work we had generated, sorting through it, and compiling it into what would become the training manuals. We then combed through the various drafts, refining and editing them until we were satisfied that everything cohered and was in order.

After nine months of blood, sweat, and tears, it was time to start the training.

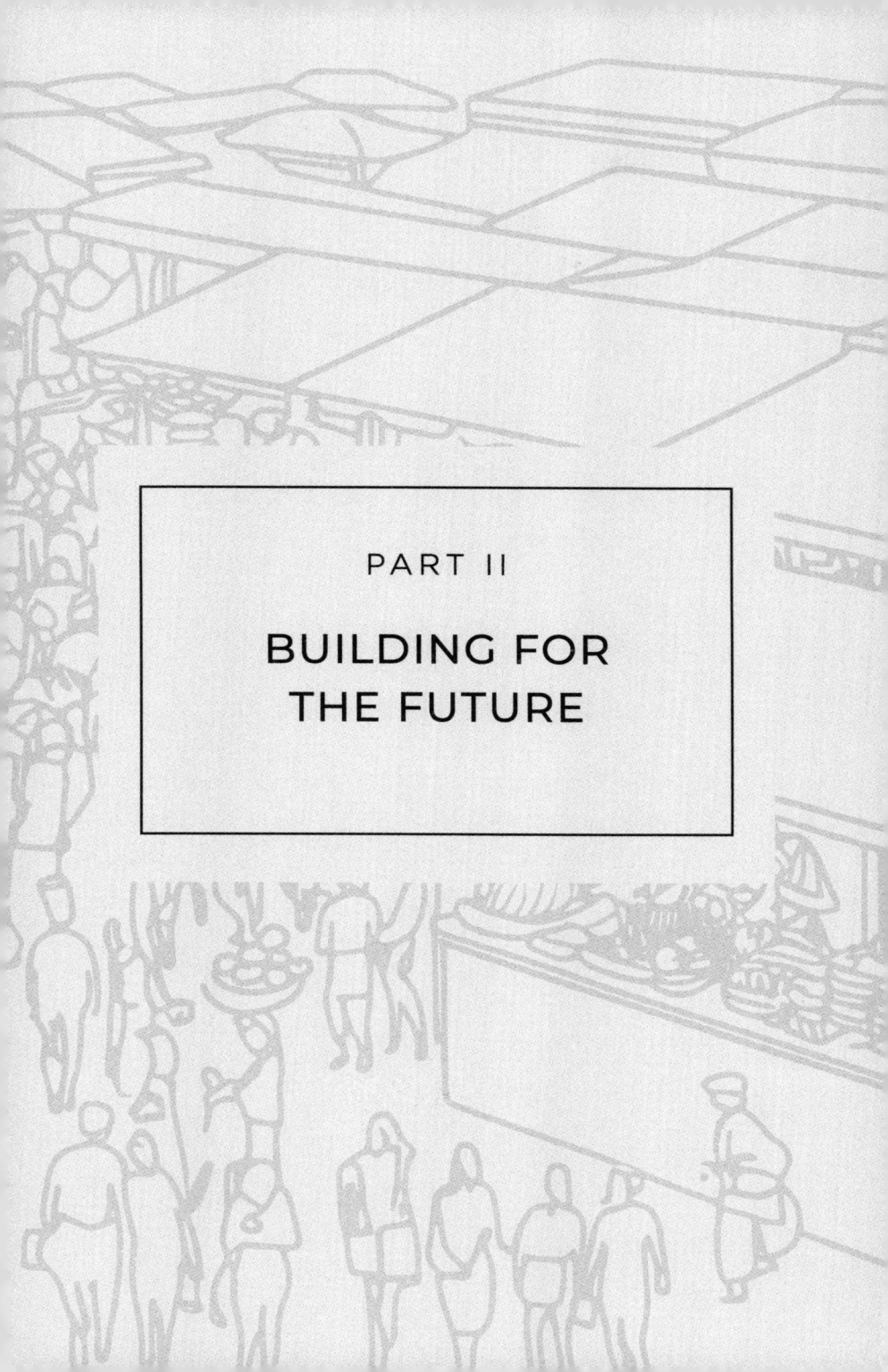

PART II

BUILDING FOR
THE FUTURE

Chapter 4

THE RISING SCHOOLS PROGRAM IS LAUNCHED

I decided to delay my own appearance at the proprietor training sessions until the program was underway. It was important that participants saw that the program was being taught by Ghanaians. Given Ghana's long, abusive colonialist past, it seemed appropriate for the Western members of the team to hang back and for us to center Ghanaian voices. Anne Hainer, however, was at every training session, and she took superb notes, which were dutifully emailed to us after every session.

While the training sessions took shape, I turned my attention elsewhere: the UN. I wanted to see what kind of support I could rally there.

MEETING AMIR DOSSAL

I had been invited to serve on the board of the Foreign Policy Association and was about to attend my inaugural board meeting in New York. On the evening of the meeting, they were offering a lecture that piqued my interest. The guest speaker was Amir Dossal, the executive director for the United Nations Office for Partnerships, who would eventually become one of my greatest supporters and facilitators.

To understand his impact, it helps to know a bit of background. In 1997, media mogul, television producer, philanthropist, and entrepreneur Ted Turner decided to donate US$1 billion to UN causes. He knew that several countries had not paid their dues to the UN, and his charitable contribution was intended to cover part of the UN's shortfall in revenue. Since the UN was technically unable to accept donations from an individual, Secretary-General Kofi Annan suggested that Turner set up a foundation and that the UN would set up an office to work with his foundation on dispersing the funds. That was the genesis of the UN Foundation, which was set up "as a strategic partner to help the UN mobilize the ideas, people, and resources it needs to deliver and grow a diverse and durable constituency for collective action." Amir was asked to head up the UN office (the UN Fund for International Partnerships), and he was giving the talk the night I was in New York. He was an excellent and engaging speaker. Afterward, I plucked up the courage to go up to him and ask him some questions about my dilemma. I told him what I had witnessed in Ghana and what I wanted to see happen with these schools. He was very responsive and encouraging. "Why don't you come to my office, and let's sit down and talk?" he asked after I'd explained.

Many meetings were to follow, some of which were attended by other senior members of his team. Our shift from traditional philanthropy toward a more strategic, sustainability-focused approach—moving away from direct aid—was a new concept for them.

They asked, "What makes you think that you can have any possible impact when all of these UN and international development agencies have been working on this problem for seventy to eighty years and haven't managed to get very far?"

"Exactly my point!" I said.

I should explain that in September 2000, the UN had set eight Millennium Development Goals (MDGs) to achieve by 2015. These were UN initiatives created through workshops in which all member states participated. Drafting them involved lots of debates and weeks and weeks of exchanging ideas and putting forward solutions. One of those goals was to achieve free universal primary education by 2015. That was Millennium Development Goal 2 (MDG 2).

At the United Nations Conference on Sustainable Development, Rio+20 in 2012, the UN recognized that the eight MDGs would never be achieved by 2015, so another series of debates began in the UN, resulting in the Sustainable Development Goals (SDGs). I observed many of these sessions over the three years during which they were created. Individual countries had their national agendas, budget constraints, and, quite often, a lack of adequate infrastructure that hindered achieving these goals within such a relatively short period. The UN also recognized that, while these goals were aspirational, they could never be achieved without the active engagement and participation of the private sector and civil society. (See Appendix A for a list of the MDGs and the SDGs.)

The SDGs were much more comprehensive than the MDGs. There were now 17 goals, 169 targets, and several hundred indicators. MDG 2 now fell under SDG 4. SDG 4 focuses on education and aims to "ensure inclusive and equitable quality education and promote lifelong learning opportunities for all."

Against this background, I suggested to Amir that we consider putting together a consortium of interested stakeholders who could provide intellectual guidance as well as expertise on the ground to further our efforts in Ghana. By then I felt I had gained a good understanding of the educational system on the ground in Ghana.

But when I continued to make this suggestion in many subsequent meetings with various organizations, it was usually met with blank stares. These were discouraging meetings. Apparently, my idea was impossible in the eyes of those with whom I met.

UNLOCKING OPPORTUNITIES, CONFRONTING OPPOSITION

"Let me start opening some doors for you," Amir said. And he did. He taught me how to navigate the UN. He showed me which agencies I needed to be talking to and introduced me to key UN delegates, choosing people with some familiarity with the issues I was working on to address. He opened door after door after door, and I was, and remain, profoundly grateful.

Whenever I met with Amir in the UN (or nearby), I would insist that he sit facing away from the room—otherwise it was impossible to have a conversation with him. Our meeting would just devolve into a nonstop series of interruptions by people wanting to come and pay their respects. He was a celebrity of sorts at the UN, and deservedly so. He encouraged me to apply for consultative status, which I received for the IDP Foundation. When you have consultative status with the UN, you have the legitimacy—and a certain credibility—to engage in panel discussions, attend conferences, have conversations with key stakeholders at the UN, make comments, and submit written statements, and sometimes you're even invited to speak. The UN in New York has five main chambers, a multitude of enormous conference rooms, and a never-ending series of activities on every imaginable subject of consequence to the UN. I found that to have a voice in these proceedings was of enormous importance to lend credibility to my work.

I walked resolutely through every door that Amir opened for me.

I learned quickly that the controversy about low-fee private schools was not confined to Ghana. For hundreds of millions of children around the world, their only shot at education was in these incredibly under-resourced, marginalized, and disenfranchised schools. Governments were largely in denial about their existence, and international development agencies only funded government schools. Most financial institutions considered low-fee private schools too risky to lend to, and furthermore, there was the publicly funded versus privately funded debate to contend with. I found the armchair academics who had no real field experience but loudly expressed their public-only ideologies the most challenging. A typical conversation with these people often went something like this:

> **Them:** "A free, publicly provided education is a universal human right."

> **Me:** "I agree. But there are fees and other expenses associated with public education."

> **Them:** "But private school education is elitist! These proprietors are taking advantage of and getting wealthy off the backs of the poor!"

Me: "I understand why you might think that. However, I've visited many of these schools. They are barely subsisting. No one is getting rich, and, yes, families that send their children to these schools are some of the poorest in the world. But they can afford the fees, which aren't significantly higher than the fees they must pay at state schools. Also, many of these low-fee private schools offer several free tuition placements to parents who can't afford to send all their children to school."

Them: "But why aren't they going to the state schools?"

Me: "Many of the schools are too far away, overcrowded, or dangerous for the children to travel to. And parents often complain that they are poorly governed with little accountability for teachers who don't show up regularly."

Them: "But the teachers in low-fee schools aren't trained at the level that state school teachers are."

Me: "That is true—but at least they are actually in school teaching. An absent, trained state schoolteacher is less useful than an untrained teacher who is actually present and accountable to the proprietor. Besides, test results from these private schools are consistently on par with or even slightly higher than the state schools."

Them: "Supporting these schools could undermine the whole state-sponsored education infrastructure."

Me: "I see your point, but what are we to do when governments simply don't have the resources to fulfill their obligation to provide a free education? These private schools *do* exist. Whether we like it or not, they are operating and growing in number, answering the very real needs of parents and students across the developing world. The idealism behind achieving a free and universal education is admirable. But speaking pragmatically, what do we do in the meantime until those ideals are reached?"

Them: "Goodness. Is that the time? I really do have to go. Thank you so much for coming in to visit."

It didn't take long to realize that despite all the doors that were opening for me to engage in conversations, those same doors shut very quickly when it came to finding support for low-fee private schools. There were no programs in place that could be adapted to help them. Any agency that only worked through the government couldn't support the low-fee private schools—because they weren't recognized or acknowledged by the government. All funding was closed to these schools.

MEANWHILE, BACK IN GHANA . . .

After so much time and so much hard work, it was hard to believe we were ready to begin. We modeled these sessions thoroughly, but putting them into action was a separate challenge.

In the three-year pilot study, we included 105 schools representing 27,000 students. We divided the proprietors into three tranches. Most of the proprietors were older. Some were retired teachers. Some were tribal chiefs, and some were education officers. Some lacked education almost entirely and could not be considered literate. Nevertheless, there was great energy in the room when we began and complete willingness to attend the training.

Each tranche of proprietors attended fifteen training sessions. The same class was taught twice a week. You weren't allowed to miss a class. If you missed Tuesday, you better make it up on Thursday. If you missed too many classes or couldn't make up the work, you wouldn't get the loan. The classes went through lunch, so we provided participants with a meal. Despite the considerable hardship it took some to get to classes, once they were there, all the proprietors were very engaged.

On Tuesday, November 3, 2009, we began our first tranche of the pilot program in the Ashanti region at the Sinapi Aba headquarters. The general focus of the classes centered around basic financial literacy and school management. They also covered learning how to be good stewards of their institutions and understanding the fundamentals of community, health, sanitation, and safety. We were trying to ensure that proprietors had the necessary knowledge and skill sets to manage their loan portfolios while improving their schools' income and structural development. The courses were deeply participatory and conducted predominantly in English but also in local dialects when necessary.

Vincent Amponsah led the classes. He was the ideal leader for the group. Not only was Vincent a loan officer for Sinapi Aba, but he had also been a teacher—and his mother was a proprietor of her own private school. In addition, he was energetic and an extremely skilled communicator who was able to engage the participants. There was laughter and applause throughout the day.

After playing a short game to break the ice at the beginning of the session, Vincent began with a discussion about income and fixed versus variable costs. He used a jar filled with small balls to represent the school's accounts. When a cost was incurred, a ball was removed; when income was documented, he put a ball back into the jar. The jar, he explained, represented profit and loss. That week's homework? Track expenses for the school and separate them into fixed and variable costs.

After lunch, there was a discussion about subsidizing school costs since most proprietors needed an additional source of income. Vincent emphasized the importance of financial sustainability, explaining how supplementary revenue could support the school until it became self-sufficient. Ensuring long-term viability was a core objective of the program—growth depended on the school's ability to sustain itself.

Next, the emphasis was on accountability, trust, and good stewardship—also necessary components for remaining in the program. This was followed by talking about the importance of medical care and first aid. In this first tranche, only three proprietors had first-aid kits available in their schools.

At the end of the day, Vincent would invite everyone to share something they had learned, often asking them to go into depth

> Crises are inevitable, the trainers told them. How one responds determines whether a school will survive.

and detail. The day ended on a bright note with all proprietors signaling their appreciation for the program. Just as with the first cohort, homework tasks were assigned.

We were off and away!

TRAINING TO TRANSFORM

The response from proprietors was remarkable. They immediately began separating their personal and business finances. And the health and safety section prompted one proprietor to get her well fixed that week, a task she had been overlooking.

In the weeks that followed, there was a robust course on basic financial literacy and lessons in how proprietors could manage their schools within the context of their communities, including crisis management.

What kind of crises did the proprietors face? The roof of one school was ripped off by a violent storm. At another, a terminally ill child had been spanked by a teacher—and then tragically died of their illness a few days later. Newspapers falsely reported that the teacher had killed the child, and the teacher subsequently resigned. One proprietor asked parents to pay their fees via a bank, which drove away almost all the parents because of added bank charges, and one school was almost completely destroyed by a fire. Another proprietor found out that his school building had once been a hideout for criminals, so parents were afraid to leave their children there.

Crises are inevitable, the trainers told them. How one responds determines whether a school will survive.

One thing I was determined to address in the training was the use of the cane. I insisted that all schools that wanted to participate in the program renounce corporal punishment. Vincent would announce at training sessions: "The donor does not condone the use of the cane or spankings." Proprietors would often recite the Bible in response: "Spare the rod, spoil the child."

"Well, regardless of that," Vincent would say, "the donor doesn't like it. There are other ways that you can instill discipline in your classrooms. As part of your homework this week, I want you to practice not using the cane. Put it away. You can use it as a pointer for the blackboard, but you're not to use it to hit your students."

The following week he asked the proprietors, "Okay, how'd it go?"

One proprietor responded, "Well, I didn't cane my student, but I did make him come and stand in front of the classroom so we all could see that he was very naughty. But all he did was stand there and pull silly faces and make everybody laugh."

Vincent responded, "Well, did you ever think about having him face the wall at the back of the room?"

Another proprietor put a bench outside her classroom, and any naughty student she felt should be punished would have to go and sit on the bench. But it was no ordinary bench. She told them it was the devil's bench. "If you sit on that bench," she told her students, "you're going straight to hell." Needless to say, parents were coming to her and asking, "Why is my child sitting on a bench that's sending him to hell? Just cane him."

Clearly, more work would have to be done to work through the cultural norms on how to instill positive discipline in the classroom.

This became a major focus of mine and would drive me to support the development of future training modules on positive discipline that are still being accessed by new partners such as UNESCO to incorporate in their teacher training.

The proprietors were also excited to be in communication with one another and shared common questions and concerns. The peer-to-peer learning was some of the most valuable training to come out of the sessions. For instance, proprietors might discuss how to respond to a student who was sleeping in class. Rather than punish them, they were urged to follow up with their parents. Sometimes they discovered that the child was living in an abusive environment or being prostituted out at night—and their misery was compounded by being caned for sleeping in class. Most proprietors had never experienced anything like this level of engagement with their concerns and were, I would say, surprised that someone was willing to support them and offer advice on running their schools.

They were also glad to learn that there were social service agencies to which they could appeal and which could be called upon to step in. Most were not aware of these resources prior to the training sessions. Representatives of external agencies were also brought in to speak to proprietors and teachers about the rights of children.

We also taught them about community engagement, encouraging them to go out into their communities. We told them to go visit a sick child when appropriate. "If a student hasn't been coming to school," they were advised, "go find out why. It shows the parents that you are a part of their community. In fact, by showing them that you care, you can be the glue that holds the community together." Some of these schools in more populated communities had plenty of competition. We wanted to give our proprietors an edge.

GETTING GOING

It took us three years to graduate 105 proprietors in three tranches. Every time we began with a new tranche, we applied lessons learned from the previous one in both content and training techniques. Most proprietors had no collateral, so when feasible, they signed an affidavit offering a building—often no more than an extension of their home—as collateral. Those who could provide guarantors were encouraged to do so, as it added value to the loan and reduced risk, particularly with the larger loans. Most of the loan payouts were broken into several installments, and all were monitored by the IDP Foundation staff and loan officers at Sinapi Aba.

The majority of the proprietors took loans for infrastructure, mostly for building classrooms. Some needed roofs for their current structures to prevent the interruption of instruction every time it rained. Some purchased vehicles to pick up and deliver students from surrounding towns and villages and to raise additional income by using the vehicle for ordinary commercial purposes.

We insisted that proprietors open bank accounts in the name of their schools at the beginning of the training, and we encouraged them to open personal bank accounts. Opening the business bank account was nonnegotiable. We also learned that we needed to create customized grace periods for repayment and that we needed to critically assess their previous loan history prior to engaging proprietors in the program. To prevent the proprietors from biting off more than they could chew, they had to guarantee they had no other debt. This was a requisite to gain admission to the program.

The training and provision of loans was a slow process, in part because the program was so new. But as we continued to disburse the loans, we learned a lot, along with the proprietors.

One loan recipient borrowed money ostensibly to build a three-classroom block but instead diverted the money to drill a well—and was going to use the remaining money to purchase a vehicle. The staff worked with her to complete the well but prevailed upon her to return the remainder of the money and apply for a separate, new loan for the vehicle, which she did. Some schools had difficulty making their loan repayments between harvests or during the rainy season, when parents kept their children at home. The loan officers were understanding but reminded proprietors of their training around cash flow and encouraged them to keep emergency funds to manage unexpected or seasonal circumstances. The proprietors shared this information with parents, some of whom had taken out loans themselves when they'd learned of the program.

We proceeded to get to work with our second tranche, refining the program as we went, making tweaks and adjustments. At the same time, we continued our conversation with education specialists, organizations like the World Bank, and economists in the education development community.

They'd ask us, "Well, what are these proprietors using the loans for?"

We'd respond, "Building. A lot of building is really what they want to do."

They'd ask, "Well, how is that improving education outcomes? What about curriculum development? What about pedagogy?"

By then, we had enough experience to parry those kinds of questions by talking about the important role improved infrastructure can play. In an equatorial country, putting a roof over the school so that the kids can go to school when it rains—and making the roof out of something other than corrugated tin so you can actually hear the teacher when the rain is pounding down on the roof—is important. There are multiple factors that affect educational outcomes. Improving a learning environment through improving infrastructure is just one of them. We had to start somewhere.

Proprietors were initially drawn to using loans for infrastructure improvements because they understood it would make a powerful impact on parents, directly aligning with their expectations and needs.

We also offered several loans for school buses. Getting the kids to and from school safely is key to educational outcomes. More rural schools generally served more than a single village, often serving a cluster of villages. Without transportation, some of the children would be compelled to walk a couple of miles, sometimes through bush paths where the danger of snakebites and even abduction was high. A bus solves those problems. It also generates immediate revenue for the school, which in turn reduces the length of the grace period needed before loan repayments can begin.

If we'd hired Western consultants, they would have focused primarily on test results and educational outcomes. Instead, by direct and local engagement with Ghanaians, we were able to tailor our program around the actual needs of the schools rather than some intellectual concept of what experts with no field experience felt was best for them.

That said, we did have a few hiccups. The greatest was probably this one:

We had set up a point system. Proprietors were awarded points for attendance, on-time arrival and departure, completed homework, and the quality of homework. Points were tallied during the program and could be used for access to donated school supplies. In terms of those supplies, when we interviewed them, we had asked the proprietors to list their most pressing material needs, and they obliged.

I had thought myself very clever in securing those supplies. When I mentioned the general shortage of classrooms and learning materials in the schools we were working with to an Opportunity International (OI) executive, he told me, "A member of Opportunity International has a huge trucking company that has made him very wealthy. He has started a philanthropic side business. He sends his trucks around the country collecting donated materials for schools, among other recipients. We could ask him if he would collect textbooks and then ship them over to Africa. If he agrees, he can send some pallets of textbooks along with pens, paper, and pencils."

That sounded just wonderful. I was very excited about this potential windfall of generosity.

He put me in touch with the gentleman, who was immediately supportive of the idea. "Absolutely, we will. Of course, we will," he said. "How many schools are we talking about? How much do we need?"

"Oh, we need a lot," I told him. "However much you think you can collect, we will be able to distribute."

He sent his trucks around the United States picking up supplies, which, besides textbooks, included soccer balls, toys, pop-up books, whiteboards, cups and plates, and large water-storage buckets with taps. Completely free of charge, he loaded all of it up and shipped it over to Ghana.

I was overjoyed—until the supplies arrived in Ghana, and I was informed that we had to pay exorbitant import duties before they could be released. The foundation paid the duties, of course, but it still looked like we were getting a pretty good deal.

However, Anne was now looking at a huge shipment of learning materials sitting on the wharf, and we hadn't yet given a thought to how we were going to transport them nearly two hundred miles to Kumasi, much less how we would distribute them to schools. Furthermore, the longer they sat at the wharf, the more it cost to store them—and the more likely it was that the container would be infested by rats.

Eventually, working with Raphael Akomeah from Sinapi Aba, Anne found transport to take the material off the wharf and up to Kumasi, where, of course, we now had to rent a warehouse to house everything—another cost I hadn't thought about. And then we noticed that the books were not sorted, and we had dozens of enormous pallets to process. Also, a good number of books had torn pages and were basically unusable. Once we determined which books were usable and sorted them by grade level, the team had to purchase and install shelving.

It's easy to imagine how simple it would be to receive a donation to help those in need, but the reality of implementing that change is far more complex than most realize. Anne and Raphael's experience is a perfect example of this. Initially, the materials seemed like a straightforward gift—until the logistics kicked in. Transporting the materials from the wharf to Kumasi was only the beginning. Renting a warehouse, sorting through unsorted, damaged books, and dealing with unexpected costs like shelving installation turned what seemed like a simple donation into an overwhelming task.

As the process grew all-consuming, the weight of the logistical challenges became clear. From afar, I felt helpless—unable to assist directly while Anne and Raphael were on the ground, navigating a labyrinth of hurdles. Their frustration was palpable, and their determination to never repeat the process was understandable. The reality of implementing change is far more intricate than it appears, requiring much more than good intentions.

Eventually Anne and Raphael managed to get everything separated and sorted into piles. At which point there was the problem of how to get them into the hands of our proprietors.

My first bright idea was Coca-Cola. After all, Coca-Cola has one of the biggest distribution setups in the world. They're everywhere. There are Coca-Cola outlets all over Ghana, even in areas with the least resources. "Let's go to Coca-Cola," I decided.

I called Coca-Cola's headquarters in Ghana to see if they would engage with us. Unfortunately, all philanthropic decisions at the Coca-Cola Company are made in Atlanta, Georgia.

"We'd love to help you," they told me, "but, honestly, it will take months to get an evaluation from the board. And there's no guaranteeing the answer."

We were going to have to distribute the supplies ourselves. There was further sorting to be done. Anne and Raphael began to separate supplies according to the regions and communities to which they needed to be delivered.

Once they had compiled the list of schools for each area, they would load up a rental truck and drive to that community. Whenever possible, they would choose a centralized location where the supplies could be picked up. Some proprietors arrived with their own trucks, coming long distances; others came on foot with friends and teachers to carry the boxes and materials back to their schools. We traveled directly to those schools unable to arrange pickups. Anne and Raphael were sometimes invited to present the supplies formally to the school in the presence of all the teachers and the students. On those occasions they were often greeted by cheering and wild enthusiasm—a much-needed emotional return for all their hard work.

Once everything had been distributed, the gratitude was certainly rewarding, but I had to evaluate the enormous burden I had placed on Anne and Raphael. What had I been thinking? Why on earth hadn't any of us really thought through the whole process ahead of time?

We scrapped the points program.

Around week nine of the training, Liesel and I made the trip to Ghana and dropped by a school to say hello. I made a short speech in which I expressed my genuine admiration for the proprietors' fortitude, their entrepreneurial spirit, and their passion and commitment to their schools. I also expressed my gratitude for the sacrifices they had all made to provide Ghanaian children with a decent education in a supportive environment. Finally, I applauded their success at having come so far with so little help. Then I shut up.

One of the earliest lessons I learned in Ghana was to listen carefully and stay out of sight as much as possible. So, we did just that and sat at the back of the classroom and observed.

It was thrilling to see the product of so many months of hard labor underway and eliciting such an enthusiastic response from the proprietors. They embraced learning with a voracious hunger. Their questions in class were on point, proof of how attentive they were to the lessons. There was a palpable sense of appreciation, understanding, curiosity, and, above all, engagement. It was particularly rewarding to see that the program was having an immediate impact on the participants. Proprietors were already applying the substance of the classes to their operations, and based on their comments, what they were learning was practical, applicable, and effective.

AND MEANWHILE, BACK IN THE CLASSROOM . . .

As educational outcomes were important to us, around the same time as we began our training programs, we administered the Primary 2 and Primary 4 standardized tests so kindly provided by the Ghana Education Service (GES). By the end of the pilot program, we had tested all the primary grade students in all 105 schools, which had a total enrollment of 27,000 children. Thomas Coleman, the coordinator for Education Monitoring Information Systems (EMIS), told me that I needed to make sure there was a proctor present during the exams because otherwise most teachers would just put the answers up on the blackboard. How did they know this? On occasion, an entire class being tested would fill in the same incorrect answer. So, we paid independent proctors to administer the tests—an expensive proposition—and then we shared the results with Stephen Adu. The kids were performing at the fiftieth percentile in reading comprehension and math, which concerned us. But then we learned from GES that children in the government schools were performing at the forty-eighth percentile. Pretty dismal performance all around.

Although the test results were low, they were at least in line with government-run schools. We believed that by helping the schools stabilize financially and improve their management, we could create a better learning environment, which would, in turn, lead to improved test scores.

It's worth mentioning again that we were learning a lot—at every stage of the process. As we received feedback from the proprietors, we continuously adjusted our playbook. We reduced the training modules from sixteen sessions to twelve sessions and then to nine sessions without negatively affecting outcomes. Another significant change: We had initially refused to provide a loan to any proprietor until they had completed the training program. But we altered that almost immediately when one proprietor—Lily Baah, who you'll get to know better later—had to get her bus repaired and was in crisis. We discovered that giving out a loan during the process of training did not affect repayment. The training was so useful that proprietors told us they were able to implement what they learned immediately. Also, they had more incentive to attend the training because, having received a loan, they were obliged to repay it; they were also more motivated to sort out their business affairs.

Upon reflection, I think it was very important that Liesel and I remained hands-on, particularly in those early days. Although the foundation was based in Chicago, as the program developed, we realized that we needed to be in Ghana more often. So, we made numerous trips, making sure that we were on the ground, visiting schools, and attending training. Because of the way our foundation was structured as a 501(c)(3) corporation with me as its sole director, we were able to respond quickly and efficiently to concerns as they arose and not be encumbered by board delays. When we couldn't be there, our staff representatives were, and we responded promptly to their texts and emails.

I don't, as a rule, like to convene endless meetings trying to perfect an idea before implementing it. If an idea is sound, I prefer to respond quickly, implement it, and then refine the idea as we go. The important thing was to get proprietors what they needed when they needed it so they could continue the important work of running their schools.

At the conclusion of the pilot program, the loan repayment success rate was remarkably high—between 90 and 93 percent. We were thrilled. But as we worked to solidify the program, we also had to address pedagogy. The proprietors were learning a great deal. But what were we to do about the untrained teachers? What came next surprised and delighted us all.

BUILDING FUTURES: A STORY OF A SCHOOL PROPRIETOR

MAGDALENE SACKEY

Phiga School (Accra, Ghana)

Magdalene Sackey's Phiga School started as a small canopy outside her mother's home, held up by a few posts with a wooden partition to divide the space. It wasn't much, but it was enough for her three children and three others to begin their education. One stormy day, the cloth that made up the roof tore apart in the wind and rain, leaving the children in tears and their parents demanding to see the damage. "I said, 'There's my building!'" she recalls, pointing to the torn fabric.

She had always wanted to open a school but lacked the financial means to make it happen. When she finally took the leap, she and her husband used their salaries to support it. Eventually, she was able to rent an apartment for the school, but expansion seemed out of reach until Sinapi Aba's Rising Schools Program found her. At first, she resisted, wary of financial institutions, but after persistent outreach, she agreed to attend the training. "I had fun. I never regretted going," she says. "When I got home, I told my husband, 'I think this will change our lives.'"

The training reshaped how she handled money. Before, she thought she understood banking and savings, but she hadn't been disciplined. "It's not all about keeping money here and there. You need to be disciplined if you want to move forward." Within a month of applying what she learned, she had saved enough to buy the school's first bus—without a loan. The structure the program provided allowed her to take out loans strategically, building Phiga School into a three-story complex over time.

Funding remains her greatest challenge. When parents struggle to pay tuition, it strains everything. She needs good teachers, and they must be paid well. She has over thirty staff members depending on her, and she is deeply committed to them. "Let me use the word 'amazing,'" she says of her teachers. She fosters a strong sense of belonging, telling new hires, "We are a family! The parents, the teachers, the children—we are a big family."

She wishes the government recognized the role private schools play in the nation's education system. At one time, all registered schools received government textbooks, but over the years, those resources dried up. "The government cannot build all the schools for the nation. Private schools are easing the burden." Still, Phiga School thrives. It won the Greater Accra spelling bee, and high school teachers regularly call to praise the preparedness of its graduates.

Her vision has only grown. She recently purchased four acres of land to open a vocational academy, ensuring that every child who comes through Phiga School leaves with the skills to pursue a career of their choice. The Rising Schools Program gave her business stability. Now, she has the space to dream.

Chapter 5

ADDRESSING PEDAGOGY
WITH SESAME WORKSHOP

While we focused on training school proprietors to build sustainable businesses, ensuring long-term success also required improving the quality of teaching. I remained firm in my belief that setting a teaching curriculum was a job best left to the government. However, the quality and style of teaching in the schools that made up the Rising Schools Program was an issue that had to be addressed.

Some common barriers mitigated against child-friendly learning environments in most of the schools with which we were engaging. These included the widespread practice of corporal punishment as well as a lack of physical and social accommodation for girls and children with mental and physical disabilities. The lack of professional development resources to help teachers address these and other obstacles was having a direct impact on the quality of education in the schools in our program.

We set out to create a teacher training manual that would move untrained teachers beyond rote instruction and bring new energy to their classrooms.

We were familiar with a man who had written a teacher's textbook for primary grade levels, and we thought that perhaps he could write a series of teaching training modules for us and that we could get the government to sponsor training for our teachers. We were, of course, completely wrong on both points. The government had policies that made it difficult to extend teacher training. Due to political reasons and pressure from the teachers' union, it refused to subsidize free state-sponsored training for our teachers. At the same time, it was subsidizing untrained public school teachers who were working toward certification. Even though the government collected taxes from the poorest school proprietors, it still denied low-fee private school teachers a pathway to certification.

Meanwhile, the Ghana Education Service (GES) *was* willing to share its curriculum, and they sent over an electronic copy of it for all grades, from primary school through junior high school. But the problem was that it wasn't broken into any programmatic scheme. The government curriculum had a full-on syllabus for each subject, with concentrations on reading, writing, and arithmetic. So at least we had our hands on that.

Despite being highly recommended, the man we had hired to write a textbook on the principles of teaching and the subject matter for a teacher's handbook was unable to deliver a usable manual. He held a one-week live-in training session with some of the teachers just to talk about the importance of teaching, but it was a huge waste of time, money, and effort. He was disorganized, the training was boring, and, consequently, the teachers were uninspired. We handed out certificates to our untrained teachers at the conclusion of the workshop, which they very much appreciated, though they were only ceremonial and held no value. We had generated some goodwill with our efforts, but I was discouraged and thought, *There's no way to solve this.*

But I was wrong.

Just as I was beginning to despair that we would never crack this nut, Amir Dossal suggested that Liesel and I join an organization called Synergos (Greek for "working together"). It was founded by Peggy Dulany, David Rockefeller's daughter. Synergos was very good at securing support for projects they wished to sponsor that addressed poverty, social injustice, or climate change. I was at a roundtable session at their annual meeting at which Peggy interviewed both the CEO and the head of development at Sesame Workshop.

Sesame Workshop is the nonprofit organization behind Sesame programming, the remarkable and groundbreaking television show that has been teaching children since its inception in 1969. It is active in more than 150 countries.

The CEO highlighted the organization's powerful impact, sharing how their programs didn't just educate—they changed minds. One striking example was Kami, an HIV-positive Muppet designed to break down stigma and foster understanding in a world that often turned away from those facing her reality. Her character premiered in 2002 on the South African version of *Sesame Street—Takalani Sesame.* The CEO explained how hard they had worked to change the mindsets of people using Muppets.

As an example of their success, the workshop group had in tow some of the kids they'd brought together during the Northern

Ireland crisis by explaining differences in religions. As I sat there thinking about rote learning and cane-swishing, suddenly, this lightbulb went off, and I thought, *My God, if anyone can change the attitude of how teachers view their role and help raise their self-esteem and see a new way to approach teaching, it will be Sesame Workshop! They make everything fun.*

And this "lightbulb moment" was how the Sesame Pedagogy Program came to be.

Shortly after the presentation, I called Sesame Workshop with a project in mind. When we met, I painted a stark picture of classrooms in Ghana, showing photos of severely underprivileged schools and describing the harsh reality: children being routinely whacked with a cane. The only teaching model these educators knew was the one they had experienced themselves—rote memorization, parroting lessons, and reciting back information without true understanding.

As we began working with the Sesame team, I outlined the key challenges these schools faced with their pedagogical approach. After extensive classroom observations, I detailed the critical topics we needed to address. "These are untrained teachers," I explained. "How do we inspire them to teach with creativity and positivity? They're paid below the basic wage because most have only a high school education. Many never attended college due to financial constraints. How do we help them transform classrooms into spaces where students aren't just chanting lessons but are truly engaged? And with so few teaching resources, how do we equip them to be effective educators?"

Sesame Workshop embraced the challenge, and we formed a partnership. They assigned dedicated staff to the project, and I was immediately struck by their professionalism. They were always on time, were always on budget, and brought in brilliant writers. Every aspect of their operation ran like clockwork, with each team member seeing their work through from start to finish. We were deeply impressed by their commitment and expertise.

CRAFTING CULTURALLY RELEVANT CONTENT
FOR GHANAIAN TEACHERS

Our goal was to create a series of training videos and two training manuals—one for teachers and one for teacher trainers. Each teacher would receive ten DVDs and a manual.

Most of the programming was created at the regional office of Sesame Workshop in Nigeria, and the main teacher to be featured in the video series would be Nigerian. But as Nigeria and Ghana are very different culturally, we thought it important to have a Ghanaian teacher, too. Believe it or not, I still encounter the colonial mentality that leads people to assume that all African nations are basically the same, even though they wouldn't dream of making that assumption about countries in Europe.

Ayobisi Osuntusa was hired to be the project lead. She lived in Abuja, Nigeria, and owned a private school where she was also a teacher. She also worked for Sesame Workshop, so she was an ideal collaborator on the project.

Sesame Workshop, with its long-standing company philosophy of learning through play, was the perfect partner to find a way to counteract the rote learning and drudgery of memorization. They warmed up to the task of creating material for teachers that directly addressed classroom discipline by focusing on answering questions and assigning homework rather than relying on humiliation, fear, and the cane.

I gave them the topics I thought needed addressing, and they got to work writing the scripts. It was amazing to experience it all coming together.

We went to Lagos in Nigeria. I read every script first and then gave it to the Ghanaian team to look for cultural modifications because, as I previously stated, Nigeria is not Ghana. But since we wanted the modules to be available to teachers in both countries, there was some balancing of cultural sensitivities that needed to be done. We decided that we would use existing Muppets from the Nigerian show *Sesame Square*: Kami (who we mentioned earlier) and Zobi.

I also asked if the setting for the school they used in the videos would closely resemble the kind of schools in our program, to be relatable, so the teachers would see themselves in these videos.

Each video leveraged Sesame Workshop's lovable, engaging Muppets and their unique ability to reach both children and adults. In the video modules, the Muppets ask questions and share the same concerns that children face daily in classrooms, from academic learning of literacy and numeracy to social skills like understanding differences and extending empathy to other children, and, especially for girls, developing self-confidence.

It was an expensive venture. The initial proposal from Sesame Workshop was to create twenty modules, but we decided that fourteen modules would encompass all that we wanted to impart and fit within our budget.

The fourteen videos supported:

1. The fundamentals of teaching
2. Developing a child-friendly learning space

3. Positive discipline and classroom management
4. Developing and teaching with creative, low-cost resources
5. Pupil-centered learning for English literacy
6. Pupil-centered learning for mathematics
7. Time management
8. Practical ways to make the classroom creative and fun
9. Differentiated instruction
10. Evaluation and assessment
11. Girls' education and inclusion in the classroom
12. Ensuring an inclusive learning environment
13. Early education and child development
14. Learning through play

To be on set with the Muppets and the Sesame Workshop team is inspiring. A good deal of the filming was done in South Africa, but I was able to sit in on some of the filming in Nigeria. It was fascinating to watch the Muppeteers at work filming the modules. I hadn't realized how many different types of Sesame puppets there are and how many people it takes to bring them to life. There are some for which you only see their faces and some that have arms as well that wave around and require separate Muppeteers. One Muppeteer sits with their legs in a V, and the other squats upright inside the other to make two Vs. One of them has a head and operates the mouth, the other the arms. And when you operate the head, only the bottom jaw moves, mimicking the way people speak. The Muppeteers work underneath the set so that only the puppet is on camera. The way that they coordinate with one another is absolutely extraordinary. It looks effortless on screen, but

I can unequivocally say that it's extremely difficult to be a Muppeteer, but the whole process is a lot of fun. Our arrangement with Sesame Workshop allowed us to put the videos up on our website and YouTube.*

The module videos begin and end with interactions between Muppets Zobi and Kami and a winsome teacher, Ms. Efia, played by a Ghanaian celebrity. Ms. Efia's classroom was lively, colorfully decorated, and welcoming. "I help children learn how to succeed and how to be happy," she says in the "Fundamentals of Teaching" video. "In my classroom, my pupils learn how to be good thinkers and good citizens."

Zobi and Kami ask questions, comment on Ms. Efia's classroom, and share concerns, leading into scenes of teachers in actual Ghanaian classrooms demonstrating techniques relating to module topics that are augmented with voiceover takeaways.

In "Practical Ways to Make the Classroom Creative and Fun," Zobi and Kami play a new song for their favorite teacher, Ms. Efia, slapping out the rhythm on a drum. "You know," Ms. Efia points out, "you can use numbers to play your rhythm [and] your eyes and ears to count the beats."

"How about," she suggests, "instead of using boom-boom-boom, use numbers?" Zobi and Kami are all in, delighted with Ms. Efia's improvisational twist.

After the opening sequence, with Zobi and Kami jamming with Ms. Efia, the scene shifts to a class in Ghana where the teacher is encouraging hands-on interactive learning and

---

* For those interested in viewing, you can still find these videos at: https://www.idpfoundation.org/sesame-workshop/modules.

experimenting with new ways to teach the standard curriculum. The teacher, having noticed that several pupils were interested in birds outside the school, invites his class to speculate about how big a parrot's nest would have to be and what types of materials are needed to build it. Outside they gather twigs, grass, strings, and other materials, then they imagine they are birds and write stories about building their nests. Finally, they act out the stories for their peers.

Each video contains several powerful messages. One of my favorites is the "Learning through Play" video, which begins with Zobi and Kami pretending to be taxi drivers. Ms. Efia reaches into her box of classroom supplies to provide them with colorful leis for seat belts and "super speedy" steering wheels (paper plates). Zobi fancies himself an explorer, with a pair of binoculars fashioned out of cardboard tubes from rolls of toilet paper.

Later, a teacher asks a young pupil, Kofi, to name a job that he'd find exciting. "A pilot!" Kofi beams before the teacher leads a hands-on project making and flying paper airplanes, which becomes a lesson incorporating design, shapes, and measurement.

"Let children contribute ideas to help make your lessons more playful," the video suggests. "They'll be even more involved if you build things around their interests." It ends with Zobi and Kami excitedly musing about pretending to fly a rocket ship, drive a bus, or build a house or sailboat.

"Tomorrow is going to be so much fun!" Kami exclaims.

Each video offers a vibrant demonstration of creative, engaging ways that teachers can work with young pupils. By showcasing moments from underserved Ghanaian classrooms led by exemplary teachers—paired with thoughtful voiceover takeaways—viewers gain practical insights into effective teaching, creating child-friendly learning spaces, managing classrooms and time, and making the most of low-cost resources.

Along with the video modules and the manuals, we had live teacher training sessions. First, the Sesame Workshop team trained the trainers, and then the trainers trained the teachers. The program was called Techniques for Effective Teaching (TFET).

The TFET modules aren't intended to replace the existing curriculum but work within it to provide more effective ways to make topics engaging. They're meant to demonstrate ways to create classroom environments that feel joyful and playful through the interaction of children and teachers.

The extent of the engagement of teachers during the in-person training was remarkable. The way that Sesame trains is through demonstration, so teachers experienced the training directly. It's all about making school fun. How do you, above all else, raise the self-esteem of a teacher? How do you show a teacher just how incredibly important they are in a child's life and how they—more than anybody—can actually influence the way a child grows and learns and gets excited about things?

"I try very hard to make sure that my students enjoy school," Ms. Efia explains in one video. "And do you know what else? I enjoy it, too. In fact, I love being a teacher. I'm very proud of the work I do."

The proprietors were delighted, and the modules received several ringing endorsements.

"As soon as we recruit teachers, I take them through the Sesame training, because I attended the Sesame Street workshop myself," said Paa Willie, from the Kumasi Region. "We also show them the videos, which teach them how to also control their classrooms."

TRANSFORMATIVE RESULTS

When school proprietor Rebecca Amoako signed up for the TFET program, little did she know how personally the training would touch her. Module 12 in particular, "Ensuring an Inclusive Learning Environment," validated all her childhood struggles, especially those with physical and learning disabilities.

"I was a very quiet child growing up because I couldn't talk," she told me. "My parents thought I was intentionally not speaking, and my teachers did not understand me and would either make fun of me or try to force me to say something."

Rebecca was able to overcome her speech issues over time, but not before enduring years of torment and feeling misunderstood and unsupported. She withdrew and found solace in books, becoming an avid reader and an excellent student.

Despite her learning difficulties, Rebecca's skills expanded as she got older. She excelled at dressmaking and, as a young adult, opened her own shop and taught other women in the community to sew. And through that, she discovered her love of teaching.

Today, Rebecca is the proud owner of her own school, Bethel RIM Preparatory School, in Cape Coast, providing education for over two hundred low-income children aged six months to thirteen years old. Her own son, who experienced similar speech difficulties, became the head teacher at the school.

Her involvement in the Rising Schools Program led her to the TFET training program. While she appreciates all the program's modules, Rebecca says she is especially grateful for the inclusive learning module because it acknowledges and addresses the challenges faced by students with special needs and exposes teachers to alternative supportive teaching techniques.

"The TFET training is the best," Rebecca said, "because there are a lot of children like me and my son out there who are not being understood and [are] neglected. Many kids would have been helped by now if we had received this training and intervention some years ago. I am going to personally ensure that this training is totally transferred to all my teachers and that every teacher that comes in will implement it going forward."

Chris Academy is another of the nearly 150 schools that have participated in phase one of the TFET program. Since incorporating the child-centered teaching techniques, the school's proprietor, Christiana Adu Kyeremeh, has witnessed significant changes.

She utilized the TFET modules and materials during the school's weekly teacher meetings and had the teachers practice together after watching and discussing the videos. Prior to participating in the TFET program, teachers at Chris Academy were not very engaged during those meetings. After incorporating TFET into the teacher development sessions, the feedback from the educators was extremely positive.

"One of the greatest benefits of enrolling in the TFET program is witnessing the change in my teachers' attitudes. They are more confident and relaxed," Christiana said.

The teaching methods are new strategies for Chris Academy teachers, and the play-based learning and child-centered techniques have improved the way that teachers instruct students and manage their classrooms. One teacher mentioned that she never knew teaching could be fun until she watched the TFET module videos and saw how to make learning exciting for everyone.

"The Sesame videos have helped my teachers significantly," Christiana says. "The instructors' skills and attitudes toward teaching have changed for the better. I have also seen positive changes in students' attitudes."

One of the teachers at the Baah Memorial School in Kumasi explained, "I remember the workshop we had that taught us how to manage our classrooms. I worried at first that when I would take the cane out of my class, I would become powerless. But through the training section, I came to realize that we, as teachers, are more powerful than the cane! So now I put the cane aside, and I am still able to control my class."

Music to my ears!

BUILDING FUTURES:
A STORY OF ANOTHER SCHOOL PROPRIETOR

LILY BAAH

Baah Memorial School (Kumasi, Ghana)

Lily Baah's journey toward opening Baah Memorial School began as a dream. Inspired by her love for children and conversations with her father about founding her own school, she spent years dreaming of a place where education could thrive despite the challenges of government-run institutions. Wanting to see more of Ghana, she started traveling. However, financial constraints kept the dream just out of reach.

Her father, always supportive, would send her pictures of others who had started private schools while she was away, reminding her to keep the dream alive. It worked. When Lily returned home, she was determined to make it a reality. Having taught at a state school herself, she understood the struggles that came with providing quality education in government institutions. Her decision to start a private school was a natural response to those challenges.

In 2005, Lily opened Baah Memorial School with only six nursery students, beginning in a small five-room house that she had built for her family. The initial setback came when a planned land purchase for the school fell through, forcing her to move her family into her mother's home and convert the house into a school. She took to the streets to promote the school but faced major disappointment when only six children showed up despite sixty being registered. "I nearly stopped. Why didn't they come?" she recalls. Determined, she offered to cover costs like uniforms and even accepted plantain or cassava as payment.

Slowly, her school began to grow. She worked tirelessly, doing everything from bathing children and cooking meals to acting as the janitor and accountant. Even as she struggled to fix a broken school bus, she continued to push forward. But by 2009, Lily realized she needed help, especially with the growing debt and the constant demands on her time. That's when she found the Rising Schools Program.

In tears, she approached Sinapi Aba's loan program. "It came in very handy," she says, describing how the program helped her develop better financial management skills, making her business operations smoother. Despite the program's policy requiring training before loans were disbursed, Lily's situation was urgent, and Sinapi Aba released her loan early. This allowed her to fix her bus and continue expanding the school, which now served 195 students by 2010.

The success of Baah Memorial School did not come easily. With consistent loans from the Rising Schools Program, Lily expanded the school's infrastructure, building additional classrooms and adding grade levels. She was able to provide her students with a quality education, even offering a boarding program for students who lacked power and internet at home. This dedication was reflected in her students' success, as many went on to excel in secondary schools and universities.

Today, Lily continues to mentor other school proprietors, paying forward the support she received from the program. Baah Memorial School's enrollment has grown from 195 in 2010 to 566 in 2019, a testament to Lily's resilience, hard work, and dedication to providing quality education in her community.

Chapter 6

FACING CHALLENGES

The Rising Schools Program was in business. The pilot program took three years to complete, evolving through three tranches, one per year, and each tranche was shaped and refined as we progressed. When the third tranche was completed, it was clear that the program was going to succeed. The repayment rate stood at 97 percent, and feedback from proprietors was tremendously positive. The foundation was functioning well, and as the Rising Schools Program expanded, we started to add more staff.

I continued to direct the program, supported by Anne. She had originally been hired as an administrative assistant for the foundation just before we started the pilot program, and she proved to be invaluable. I promoted her to work full-time as program manager. I am deeply grateful to her for her early support of the program.

Anne needed to hire her own assistant, as the program was expanding quite rapidly. She brought in a brilliant young woman, Allison Lawshe, who had a bachelor of arts in economics from the

University of Wisconsin, a certification in essentials for human resources from Northwestern University, and a master of public policy from the University of Chicago.

Someone also needed to oversee the legal and compliance issues—essentially the operations of the foundation. I was lucky enough to find another brilliant woman, Alison Ehlke, who had a bachelor of arts in geography, travel, and tourism from St. Cloud State University in Minnesota and an applied business certification from the University of Minnesota.

Meanwhile, Raphael Akomeah was working for Sinapi Aba full-time on the Rising Schools Program, and the IDP Foundation was underwriting his salary. Raphael had an accounting degree from Kumasi Polytechnic, a bachelor of business administration in finance and banking from Christian Service University College in Kumasi, and a master of financial management from Amity University in India.

It was an impressive team.

Meanwhile, in between our numerous trips to Ghana to observe trainings and visit schools, we took on the essential job of spreading the word about the success of our pilot program.

BUILDING AWARENESS:
PROMOTING THE RISING SCHOOLS PROGRAM

The team organized an Education Stakeholders' Conference in Ghana. It was a collaboration between the IDP Foundation, DFID (the UK Department for International Development), and UNESCO (the United Nations Educational, Scientific, and Cultural Organization). The meeting was held on October 18, 2011, at La Palm Royal Hotel in Accra, Ghana. The stakes were high, and the team prepared for months. Our goals were straightforward: We wanted to bring together government officials, development partners, non-governmental organizations (NGOs), and other key stakeholders in education to highlight the importance of low-fee private schools in the educational space and to promote opportunities for improving access and quality through public–private partnerships. But given the tensions that existed between the public and private sectors, it was anyone's guess as to whether we would succeed—and whether anyone would show up.

When the big day came, we all held our breath and set out for the hotel. We were more than relieved to see that we had seventy attendees from various walks of life. A significant number of the attendees were government officials, which made the stakes even higher. With our programs on the line, we had to succeed.

We were lucky enough to have convinced Stephen Adu, the director of basic education and acting deputy director-general at Ghana Education Service (GES), to open the event. He gave an excellent speech stating the overall goals of the conference, which included examining research into the ever-expanding low-income private-school sector and exploring the current state of education in Ghana. He encouraged attendees to focus on collaborative solutions toward achieving the UN Education for All goals by considering the advantages of collaboration between the public and private sectors. We all crossed our fingers in the hopes that participants would join us in taking the leap.

Our next speaker was the Honorable Deputy Minister for Pre-Tertiary Education Elizabeth Amoah-Tetteh. She gave a rousing keynote address during which she emphasized the improvements Ghana has made in recent decades in expanding access to education.

I worried that she might try to push aside the existence of low-fee private schools. However, she forged ahead, stressing the challenges that lie ahead and the private sector's potential for meeting those challenges. Not only that, but she also noted the growing number of private schools in Ghana, pointing out that there were roughly fifteen thousand private schools in 2009, with around six thousand of them being low-fee private schools. Like Stephen Adu, she encouraged all stakeholders present to consider the possibilities of collaboration between the public and private sectors to achieve the Education for All goals, the Millennium Development Goals (MDGs), and Ghana's own education objectives. We couldn't have asked for a better speech.

Ernest Dzandu followed Minister Amoah-Tetteh. Ernest, as executive director of CDC Consulting, had led a team that studied the state of public–private partnerships and education in Ghana. The study for the International Finance Corporation (IFC) sampled 136 schools in and around Accra and Kumasi in 2010, assessing the state of private education in the country, with a focus on the financial, educational, and advisory needs of low-cost private schools. He pointed out that registration of private schools had never been standardized by the GES on a regional and district level. However, most of the schools described in his report had significant longevity, demonstrating that they had been meeting the needs of communities and responding to strong market demand.

It was my turn next, leading a panel discussion that I hoped would result in a robust conversation. I had a strong lineup: Stephen Adu; Christian Koramoah, financial controller of GES; and Dr. Rachel Hinton, human development advisor for the UK Department for International Development.

Stephen was just terrific. He provided context, explaining that private schools had a long history in Ghana—since before colonial times, in fact. He described the different types of private schools, some of which were opened by philanthropists, some by communities, and some by individuals. It was clear to him that categorizing private schools was necessary. He also candidly admitted that the government was trying to support private schools (as constitutionally required) but was currently unable to provide textbooks given the realities of the national budget. However, the government did provide tax exemptions for purchasing teaching and learning materials.

Christian Koramoah, the next speaker, concerned me a little at first when he stated, "Private schools operate as private enterprises for private gain, and state money cannot be put into private persons' pockets." But he acknowledged, "We do need to consider the policies guiding education and how the government can contribute to an effective public–private partnership."

"How would a public–private partnership in education look in your estimation?" I asked. "Can we make it happen?"

"We would need budget lines to support a long-term relationship between the private sector and the state," he responded. "However, first, this idea would have to be made into an integral part of the national Education Act." It was a very realistic perspective but also completely improbable.

The next panelist to present was Dr. Hinton. "Ghana has been making big strides with private schools," she said. "About eighty-five percent are registered with the government, whereas for comparison, in Lagos, Nigeria, only around forty-five percent of low-fee private schools are registered."

Dr. Hinton continued, "We have to consider the growing private sector and discuss the options we do have, such as providing access to credit for private schools."

The rest of the day unfolded with equal success. I was so proud of the great job my team had done. They brought the right people to the table, and as a result, we had a room full of engaged participants.

Later that day, Dr. Josiah Cobbah, the head of administration at the Ghana Institute of Management and Public Administration (GIMPA), initiated one of two working group sessions to discuss key questions regarding the framework for an effective public–private partnership. The groups generated ideas of ways the private sector could add value to education, including special needs schools, teacher professional development, regulation, and accountability.

Tirso Dos Santos, the country representative for UNESCO's West Africa Cluster Office, moderated an afternoon panel discussion focusing on innovations to improve teaching and learning. His panelists included representatives from the Ghana Education Staff Development Institute (GESDI), Worldreader, Open Learning Exchange Ghana (OLE), TechAide, and Discovery Channel Global Education Partnership (DCGEP).

The last session of the day, again led by Dr. Cobbah, was a working group introduced by Ruby Sandhu-Rojon, resident coordinator of the United Nations Development Program (UNDP). At the end of the session, which focused on how the public and private sectors could partner to meet Ghana's educational goals, each table presented two or three "action" items that could be implemented to foster better public–private coordination and support. All the groups agreed that the public–private partnership needed clear policy guidelines and budget allocations. Other takeaways included proposals to fund research on our specific education space so that the government might redesign the categorization of private schools and to develop an empowered government task force to create terms of reference and measure goals and milestones to promote public–private collaboration in education.

The conference was a resounding success. Many of the people attending were exposed for the first time to the reality of the world of private schools, to their scale and variety. Before our meeting, many of the attendees assumed that private schools were all elitist, profit-making ventures. Many participants were not aware that some of the types of schools in our program even existed. Though we still had miles to go before we could expect to see a shift in government policy, we brought considerable attention to the success of our program and made a huge step toward bridging the seemingly unfathomable gap in the debate between public and private. The challenge ahead lies in continuing to provide evidence that our program could work, be sustainable, and be worthy of duplication in other markets.

Due to Amir Dossal's advocacy, I had managed to create excellent relationships with the various education programs at the UN. In 2012, I was invited to Paris to speak to UNESCO at the launch of the Global Education Monitoring (GEM) Report. This is an annual report that focuses on different aspects of education. That year, the report was a collaboration between the World Bank and the International Monetary Fund. UNESCO, in addition to monitoring World Heritage Sites, works to bring countries closer together and promotes the sharing of ideas.

My remarks were, to say the least, controversial. Here is an excerpt from my speech:

I want to challenge you today to reconsider our approach to educating sixty-one million children still out of primary school, because obviously what we have been doing is falling far short of our goals. I may upset a lot of you, but I am asking you to be generous of heart and consider thinking with a different approach to educating the world's poorest to give them an equal chance.

Confucius said, "When it is obvious that the goals cannot be reached, don't adjust the goals; adjust the action steps."

Absolutely, education should be free and provided by governments. Absolutely, education is a universal human right. The unfortunate reality is that if we continue in the way we have been, the Education for All goals will not only not be met by 2015, but it is also very likely they will never be met.

Two hundred fifty million children still do not have the foundational skills they need—the ability to read, write, and count well—without which youth will never develop transferable technical and vocational skills.*

To deal with reality, we need to expand our thinking beyond current methods of funding basic education, and we need to take a long, hard look at how tens of millions of very poor people all over the world are trying to take education into their own hands to create and fund schools

---

* United Nations Educational, Scientific and Cultural Organization (UNESCO), *Education for All Global Monitoring Report 2011: The Hidden Crisis – Armed Conflict and Education*, EFA Global Monitoring Report (Paris: UNESCO, 2011).

within their villages. If governments and aid were reaching these children, these parents would not do this.

Despite the billions of dollars dispensed in educational aid by the UN and corporations and multilateral funders, there has been a universal explosion of schools established by retired teachers and other members of deprived and unreached areas to serve the children in their communities.

The efforts of these parents and school owners are rarely factored into the funding and policy equation. But this is where we should be looking. To reach all children, we need to start coming from the bottom up, right in the villages, right where the children are never otherwise reached. We need to include, we need to empower, and we need to support this sector as part of the overall educational policy of a country.

Now this is definitely not a popular approach. "What?" say people. "Extract fees from the desperately poor? This is not the direction to go."

But as a private foundation, this is where we had flexibility and unconstrained freedom to invest risk capital to take a hard look at this sector.

And this is what we found with 105 schools that entered our pilot program in Ghana: far from profiting, these school owners barely eked out a living. The parents who chose these schools often did so because they were either the same cost or only slightly more expensive than the "free" government schools, but with the added value of being available when sometimes there was no government school, of having teachers actually present, better oversight within the school, and smaller class sizes.

We found that it is possible for a bank to extend capital in the form of loans to these schools and expect full repayment as long as there are carefully created modules of training in financial literacy and school management. Testing this market in a widespread way has been unprecedented because it was deemed too risky. We proved it isn't.

This led to an increase in the quality of the infrastructure and governance, thereby increasing both enrollment numbers and the number of days in school.

To raise awareness of the program and encourage its replication by other NGOs and in new markets, I delivered variations of this speech countless times over the years, speaking at venues across the globe, including: the Summit on Philanthropy at Forbes; as a panelist at a Social Enterprise Conference for Harvard Business School; in New York on a panel with former prime minister of the United Kingdom Gordon Brown; as part of the Speaker Series at the Yale School of Management; in Zurich at the Global Schools Forum; at the TBLI Conference held in cooperation with the Kellogg School of Business; in Beijing at the China Philanthropy Forum; at the Global Education and Skills Forum Dubai; for the Sabanci Foundation in Istanbul, Turkey; and at the APEC Women Leadership Forum. Just to name a few. But I really had no idea whether I was reaching anyone, and it wasn't until the last few years that I've seen the effects of all this advocacy.

Convincing global aid agencies that the private sector can enhance the work of the public sector continues to be a great challenge. The idea behind the Rising Schools Program has not been to replace government but to work *with* government to provide education to fill the gap until government schools can serve the whole population. The ideal of Education for All may be decades away from being realized, but I believe that we have found workable means to improve the situation in the meantime.

Of course, for governments to admit that low-fee private schools are a necessity is to admit that they are failing in their obligations, so it has been difficult to get them to publicly support our work. Perhaps one of the many reasons I have loved working in Ghana so very much is that the Ghanaian government has been an ally from the outset, and despite the occasional setback, they are to be commended for their courage in facing up to challenges.

THE EVOLUTION OF SINAPI ABA

Our greatest ally throughout the creation of the Rising Schools Program has been Sinapi Aba Trust (SAT). One of the most significant challenges we faced early on was the transformation Sinapi Aba had to undergo in order to continue growing and serving its clients effectively. When we first partnered with them, SAT operated solely as a credit-issuing trust and was unregulated by the Bank of Ghana. But in 2011, it began the demanding process of splitting into two entities: SAT, for nonfinancial activities, and Sinapi Aba Savings & Loans (SASL), for financial operations. By late 2012, SAT had moved all microfinancing activities to SASL, and in 2013, SASL received a savings and loan license from the Bank of Ghana and began banking operations.

The transition was significant. Sinapi had to overhaul financial systems, upgrade technology, revise operational policies, and raise capital to meet regulatory requirements. Branches also had to be relocated to ground-floor locations with proper safes—no small feat, as many had been on upper floors of multi-level buildings.

This shift was driven by several key developments. In July 2011, the Bank of Ghana mandated that all microfinance institutions become regulated amid growing concern that some microfinance institutions (MFIs) were exacerbating financial hardship—making risky loans to over-indebted clients or collapsing altogether, devastating communities. Investor confidence plummeted.

In response, the government formed a task force, inviting Tony Fosu, CEO of Sinapi Aba, to join based on his record of integrity and SAT's strong reputation. Tony wasn't motivated by fear of regulation—Sinapi Aba had always adhered to best practices—but he saw an opportunity to offer clients more. Many needed savings accounts, which SASL could provide. We already required program participants to open business savings accounts, and Sinapi Aba could now help them open personal accounts too. Borrowers could also benefit from saving and repaying within the same institution. Some had lost their savings in failed MFIs and were unable to repay loans. Tony believed they deserved better—and that Sinapi Aba could deliver real financial stability.

Still, he and the board knew it would be shortsighted to dissolve the trust. As a regulated savings and loan, Sinapi Aba would be restricted to banking activities and barred from offering training—even as a marketing effort. Since so much of their work fell outside traditional banking, keeping the trust active was essential.

The cost of conversion was considerable, which meant that Tony had to be very careful about the bank's operations. With no surplus cash, giving a 23 percent loan to our school proprietors when the industry standard was 46 percent became impossible. And in 2012, in the middle of their conversion process, Ghana started sinking into an economic crisis, adding to the challenges Tony faced.

At that time, the most significant source of power in Ghana was the Akosombo Dam. Whenever Ghana experienced a serious drought, the water levels in the dam fell precipitously, and consequently, the entire country experienced brutal power outages. The fluctuating power grid was dubbed a *dumsor*, which means "off-on" in Akan. During the economic crisis, this situation was compounded by oil and natural gas shortages and failing equipment, and with outages shutting down industries across the country, Ghana plunged into recession. Suddenly the country was subjected to high inflation, and lending rates soared. In addition, Ghana's currency, the cedi, was devaluing rapidly. At the beginning of the Rising School Program, the cedi was on par with the US dollar, but this devaluation continued, and by the end of 2023, the conversion rate was US$1 to GHS₵15.

In 2013, because of the economic climate in Ghana, Tony flew to Chicago to engage in serious talks about how we might sustain our work. I was incredibly sympathetic to his situation, and I was also concerned about making the program more sustainable. After some discussion, we came up with what I considered to be a clever and equitable solution.

To begin moving the Rising Schools Program along the path toward full sustainability, in August 2013 we provided SAT with

US$250,000, of which US$125,000 was a grant and US$125,000 was a loan at 0 percent interest. It was a risky moment to go forward with this plan, but time was of the essence and the philosophy was sound.

Vincent Amponsah and Tony bent over backward to keep the Rising Schools Program running because they believed in it so passionately, and their passion was supported wholeheartedly by the board of Sinapi Aba, which functioned as the board of the trust and the bank. The board's compassionate nature was an important factor in giving Tony the freedom to do what was necessary. The board understood that their primary mission, as stewards of institutions, was helping the underprivileged people of Ghana. And I'd like to add that, in my experience, their integrity as an organization is unequaled.

Many bankers would have closed the program down under such difficult economic conditions. Sinapi Aba did not. We all saw the impact the program was having: the lives affected, the high loan repayment rate, and the number of schools empowered and growing.

But despite our success, we faced a serious question: Could the Rising Schools Program survive without grants? Would it ever be entirely sustainable? The future was not yet clear to me.

BUILDING FUTURES:
A STORY OF ANOTHER SCHOOL PROPRIETOR

PAA WILLIE

Paa Willie International School (Konongo, Ghana)

William Boateng, widely known as Paa Willie, didn't start as an educator. He ran a computer training school and internet café, but when technology advanced faster than he could afford to upgrade, he turned to a lasting passion—education.

His own schooling was transformed when he moved from a government school to a private one, The Gold Mines, where his brother helped him enroll. The stark difference in quality left an impression. "I loved it there," he recalls, fueling his desire to give children better opportunities.

When he discovered a rural community lacking quality schools, he acquired land and started Paa Willie International School. "Whenever I'm at the school, I feel secure; I feel happy," he says.

The early days were difficult. "I had to run small businesses on the side just to keep things running," he admits. Everything changed in 2010 when he joined the Rising Schools Program through Sinapi Aba. His first loan of GHS₵10,000 helped him transform his grade D school—adding walls, paint, and a lawn for students. More importantly, the program reshaped his financial management. "No one knows what lies ahead," he says. "I cut my budget where I can and prepare for the future."

Beyond infrastructure, he prioritizes student support. "Some are brilliant but can't afford fees. Some are orphans or from single-parent homes. I manage finances so we can assist them." His efforts have paid off—his school consistently achieves 100 percent pass rates on the BECE (the high school entrance exam), ranking among the top in the region.

Teacher quality is another focus. He personally trains educators, ensuring they complete Techniques for Effective Teaching (TFET) modules and implement techniques from Sesame Street workshops. "We make sure they are equipped to deliver," he says.

Paa Willie believes in evolving with the times. He has rebranded marketing, updated uniforms, and added a crèche for infants. He's also introducing technical and vocational training, inviting parents to teach practical skills.

Looking ahead, succession planning is on his mind. "That's why I put systems in place," he explains. "If the system works, the business can continue even when I'm not there." The Rising Schools Program helped him create structures for sustainability. "You can have a vision, but without guidelines, you cannot progress," he says. "If we make mistakes, we refresh and pick back up again."

Chapter 7

DETERMINED TO SEEK
SUSTAINABILITY

Sustainability was a vital part of the IDP Foundation's mission. It inspired and influenced every aspect of my work. The Rising Schools Program—our flagship achievement—needed to be sustainable.

Initially the program had been a three-way collaboration between the IDP Foundation, Opportunity International (OI), and Sinapi Aba. We seeded the program with a US$1.5 million grant to OI, which transferred a portion of the money to Sinapi Aba while keeping a percentage to cover its own operating expenses and the salaries of the staff members they were seconding to the IDP Foundation. This relationship remained the same through 2012. Grants continued to be made to the trust via OI to cover the costs of creating the program, the actual pilot program itself, and program monitoring and evaluation.

At the conclusion of 2012, we commissioned the Educational Assessment and Research Centre (EARC) to conduct an independent evaluation of the program. Baseline data was collected by the research firm DAK. We hoped the study would enable us to assess the program's impact on participating schools.

The survey report, released in December 2012, revealed outstanding results that highlighted the program's significant contributions: a rise in teacher salaries and school profits; enhanced school accountability efforts, including greater parent participation and the establishment of school management committees; and a higher rate of registration with the Ghana Education Service (GES).

Upon the conclusion of our three-year pilot, we were a more mature foundation. We decided that it made sense for us to work directly with Sinapi Aba. OI and the IDP Foundation parted ways amicably. We would no longer be channeling funds through OI or engaging with their seconded staff members. We would now deal directly with Sinapi Aba Trust (SAT) and hire our own staff members.

Now that the program was fully operational, it was time to look at ways to lower costs without compromising quality and content. We had started the pilot program with sixteen training sessions, or modules, which we eventually pared down.

During the pilot program, proprietors had told us in no uncertain terms that there were too many modules. As valuable as the training was, it was taking up too much of their precious time. Reducing the number of sessions was a painful process because we had put so much love and care into creating the program. We were also concerned that participants might no longer receive crucial information. With fewer modules, would the training continue to have the same impact? As we looked over the budget for the program, it became clear that if we wanted to be sustainable, we were going to have to make further cuts.

One easy fix was to remove teacher training content from the modules since the Sesame Workshop addressed teacher training with an entirely separate initiative. In addition, we initially had a significant amount of nutritional training, which included hands-on and direct training for school caterers. This was another area we could trim, creating instead training for proprietors to monitor and guide school caterers—an acceptable compromise.

During the pilot, Vincent Amponsah led most of the sessions, but clearly, he wasn't going to be able to lead all sessions in all regions. As it turned out, like Vincent, many of our loan officers were natural teachers, and others had teaching experience. It made perfect sense to us to train the loan officers to lead the proprietor training; to maximize their effectiveness, we removed components of the training that fell outside their areas of expertise. So rather than have a loan officer struggle through a subject about which they knew nothing, we provided proprietors with a list of resources should they need support in a particular area. For most (if not all) proprietors, it was a revelation to discover that a variety of governmental resources were not only free but also readily available to them. And for the key area of the pilot program that centered around child protection concerns, we were lucky enough to engage government officials to lead those sessions at concessionary rates. By the end of 2012, we were able to reduce the number of proprietor training sessions to nine.

In addition to making the program more sustainable, we also continued to refine operations.

We instituted a more detailed reporting structure. Every two weeks, the loan officer would meet with the proprietor to track their progress. They would assess their ability to make loan payments, record the date likely for repayment of their loan, and, most importantly, engage with the proprietor and see if they needed any support. This way, the loan officers really came to know their clients and understand their needs, the purpose of the loan and its impact on their schools, and how the program was affecting the way they conducted their businesses. Once all this information was collected and compiled, we had a clearer picture of the operations and needs of program participants.

To determine whether the program could be financially sustainable, we also kept track of our own operations, auditing all operational cash flow and spending by SAT related to the program. This included disbursements, repayments (principal and interest), and all operational costs. Rates for the loans were determined by the market and fluctuated between 20 and 30 percent.

Much to our relief, we did not notice any decline in the quality of the training even though we had cut a total of seven modules from the original pilot. In fact, the program was improving, and participation was growing. It was time then to scale up. We were originally in four of Ghana's regions and now expanded our reach to two additional regions—Greater Accra and the Central Region. This enabled us to now reach 479 additional schools, resulting in the disbursement of 397 loans!

Could we continue this trend? I was thrilled with the growth but had many sleepless nights worrying about its future. We weren't on solid ground yet.

THE IMPORTANCE OF LOCALIZATION

One important way of ensuring that the program would reach sustainability was giving Sinapi Aba a great deal of autonomy in running the program. It was not a difficult choice: Sinapi Aba had collaborated with me in designing it. Although we were still directing operations from Chicago, day-to-day operations of the program were entrusted more and more to Ghanaians. Responsibility was shared by the many loan officers and branch managers who led the training sessions, managed the loans, and engaged with proprietors regularly.

> While philanthropy can often provide funding and support services, true impact comes from localization—listening, engaging, and being present on the ground. Empowering local communities with resources enables them to lead their own path forward with authenticity and sustainability.

At the core of our program was a belief that community members could solve their own challenges. Lately *localization* has become a buzzword for those who focus on international development, but it has always been central to our approach. We knew that there was a great deal of local expertise. Sinapi Aba contributed its cultural awareness and knowledge of how things operated on the ground, along with its expertise as a financial institution. In the meantime, we took care of the reporting structures so that Sinapi Aba could focus on the work that was really important.

This was a crucial step on the road to sustainability. If we were to pull back someday and let the program be completely operated from within Ghana, we needed to know that the Ghanaians would be prepared to take charge. To be sustainable, the program had to evolve locally and organically. This meant placing absolute trust in our Ghanaian partners, which we did.

While philanthropy can often provide funding and support services, true impact comes from localization—listening, engaging, and being present on the ground. Empowering local communities with resources enables them to lead their own path forward with authenticity and sustainability.

SECURING FINANCIAL INDEPENDENCE AND GROWTH

By 2014, SAT had completed its division into a trust and a savings and loan, meaning that it now had to maintain reserves at the Bank of Ghana to demonstrate liquidity. To help SAT achieve this requirement, the IDP Foundation took some risk and provided a US$1 million loan at 12 percent interest in local currency.

Most organizations refused to lend in local currency because if the local currency decreased in value, the lender's profit could be reduced considerably. However, as a foundation, we felt that it was important to make sure that SAT didn't suddenly find itself with the significant strain of having to repay an enormous loan at unfavorable rates due to circumstances beyond its control. In other words, we agreed to absorb the cost of any currency fluctuation risk.

During this time, fixed-deposit investments were receiving higher returns than the interest rates being given to proprietors, which meant that SASL could invest any unused balance from our loan into a fixed-deposit account that would generate income for reinvestment into the Rising Schools Program. We allowed Sinapi Aba to keep any interest they earned on the loans, which gave them an opportunity to increase their primary and secondary reserves, a requirement of the Bank of Ghana. However, we insisted that it use these funds to lend to more schools so the program might continue to grow.

A requirement of the loan to SASL entailed reaching an additional 350 schools and making a minimum of 276 loans, with a target date of June 30, 2016. A minimum repayment rate by proprietors of 88 percent was expected, and most importantly to me, at least 60 percent of the loans to the Rising Schools Program schools had to be to schools rated C, D, or unrated. Although it was important to keep A and B schools in the portfolio to keep it diverse and stable, I wanted to be sure that we continued to reach the kinds of schools by which I had originally been inspired during my first trip to Ghana. If we didn't continue to reach those down-market schools, the program would lose all sense to me. However, without a few higher-graded schools, the portfolio might not achieve sustainability. The A and B schools took out larger loans, which generated the revenue we needed to cross-subsidize Sinapi Aba's operational costs of lending to C and D schools. And with a mix of schools in training classes, the more advanced proprietors could mentor and share their experience with the schools in earlier stages of development. We maintained a 70:30 ratio of C/D schools to A/B schools.

NAVIGATING CURRENCY RISKS AND ENSURING VIABILITY

An unforeseen side effect of Sinapi Aba's transition from being solely a trust to a savings and loan became apparent around this time. Governmental banking restrictions for savings and loan institutions were more stringent, so securing loans became more complicated for our proprietors. They were now expected to be able to provide much more in the way of tangible collateral. While we all adjusted to this new reality, the number of loans being disbursed slowed down. But Sinapi Aba's loan officers rose to the challenge. They began working with proprietors at the launch of training sessions to get paperwork in place, sometimes going above and beyond to help them obtain titles to the land they were on, which remains a complex and difficult process even today. Soon the loan process began to pick up speed again.

As things stabilized, in June 2014, Anne decided to move on, and we promoted Allison Lawshe to chief programs officer. A month later, we hired our first Ghana-based consultant, Benedicta Boateng, in the newly created position of country director to help expand programming and interface with significant stakeholders, particularly in government. She received her bachelor of science degree in computer application and information systems from Iona College in New York and was the CEO of the Elex Company for sixteen years.

In 2015, a consulting firm called Capital Plus Exchange approached the foundation requesting to conduct a case study of the Rising Schools Program. They were exploring strategies for how they themselves might support lending to low-fee private schools. They conducted a review of the Rising Schools Program to evaluate whether the training program would enable additional commercial financial institutions to sustainably lend to low-fee private schools.

The review identified four key indicators of success within our program. It affirmed the following:

1. The remarkable and strong partnership between Sinapi Aba and the IDP Foundation
2. That the proprietor training was well received and sought out by low-fee private-school proprietors
3. That we had a productive and reasonable relationship with the Ghanaian government
4. That the program was financially viable enough to eventually be sustainable

In October 2016, we commissioned Results for Development (R4D) to develop a needs assessment and impact report to provide greater insight into the broader needs of low-fee private schools in Ghana.

From that report, we learned that our schools were continuing to demonstrate impressive resilience in the face of considerable challenges; that teacher quality was a significant priority both for parents and school proprietors; and that our training programs were truly enabling proprietors to acquire business acumen and expand their schools. It was again an encouraging affirmation of all our hard work.

By 2017, the program remained sustainable—and would be as long as the IDP Foundation continued to make debt investments to SAT. However, were we to cease investment in it, it would not survive. Though SAT had managed to pay back the entirety of its 12 percent loan and was continuing to expand the program by training more schools, the number of loan disbursements had been reduced.

Also, around this time, Raphael told me that he could no longer remain at Sinapi Aba. He was getting married and was going to look for a new job in Accra. Since we had been covering his salary at Sinapi Aba for years, it made sense to hire him to consult for us full-time. We matched his salary requirements, and he moved from Kumasi to Accra and got to work. As we did not have offices set up in Ghana yet, Tony let Raphael work out of the Sinapi office in Accra.

Raphael had been working with Sinapi Aba since the inception of the Rising Schools Program and had significant institutional knowledge. By this time, Sinapi, IDP Foundation, and Raphael had become a very close-knit family. We were all driven by the same commitment, determination, and passion. Raphael was able to both supervise the work of the program and lend support when necessary. Additionally, we seconded him to CapitalPlus Exchange, where he took on some significant consulting work, developing relationships with other financial institutions to help them grow school lending programs. One of his first engagements was in Kenya, where he worked with Premier Credit to create an extensive school loan portfolio. This connection would become important in the years to come.

Before continuing with a second phase of program expansion and making another investment with Sinapi Aba, my team and I felt that it was important to reengage with the Rising Schools Program "graduates" first, reestablishing contact and renewing relations with them to help us assess SAT's ability to take on another IDP Foundation loan.

Our evaluations led to several changes. We decided to increase the frequency of training from one to two days a week, which had the added benefit of increasing the cost-efficiency of the program. We also reduced the waiting time for proprietors to access their loans and made significant updates to our training questionnaires and our monitoring and evaluation processes.

Unfortunately, new-client Rising School Program loan disbursements continued to decline, causing the program to slow down. New schools weren't being brought into the fold. So, in 2018 I convened a partners' meeting, flying Tony and Vincent out to Chicago.

Tony told us that after paying off the 12 percent loan and all accrued interest, Sinapi's cash flow was low, and the balance had to be prioritized for follow-on loans to schools already in the program, whose requests were increasing with every new cycle. In addition, the interest rates on fixed deposits were much lower, removing a significant source of income for Sinapi Aba.

"Frankly, the repayment of the most recent loan was a struggle for us," Tony said. "We even missed a payment, which triggered a penalty. Obviously, this is a challenging situation for us. Sinapi Aba wants very much to keep the program running, but to do so, we just can't afford a loan at twelve percent."

After pausing for a moment, he asked, "Would you be willing to lend at five percent in local currency? I believe that not only can I keep our program going at that rate, but I should be able to convert the program to full sustainability by the end of the repayment period. And I think I will be able to reach a further two hundred schools, increasing the reach of the program to eight hundred schools. This would be your last loan."

Eventually, he convinced me. If he was correct, our goal was in sight. It wasn't an easy decision, but I reminded myself that the IDP Foundation was a private grant-making family foundation, and I could use philanthropic funds to develop a program that would eventually not be aid dependent.

OVERCOMING BANKING CHALLENGES
AND SCALING OPERATIONS

With our program scaling and sustainability within reach, we brought in new leadership to ensure we could meet the demands of the next phase. We brought in Stephen Opuni as a consultant in April 2018. Stephen had a strong grounding in education. His parents and his sister were all teachers, so he had deep personal insight into the challenges our proprietors faced. He also had a strong educational background himself: a bachelor's degree from KNUST in Kumasi and master's degrees from the University of Hohenheim in Germany and the University of Helsinki, plus a postgraduate certificate from Imperial College London. He had worked for four years as head of programs and policy with ActionAid, an organization addressing social justice, gender equality, and the eradication of poverty.

Allison Lawshe went to Accra, and she, Raphael, and Benedicta spent a week orienting Stephen and got him up and running very quickly. Fortunately, Stephen's previous job had included a lot of interactions with the ministry, so he had good relationships with key players.

In May 2018, after nearly four years working for the IDP Foundation, Benedicta decided to move on. She had been very effective in her role, but to our great sorrow, she unexpectedly became very ill and died a few months later.

By this point, we had reached more than 580 schools, with 190 schools servicing loans at a 90 percent repayment rate, and in April of 2019, we approved a loan to SAT for US$1.5 million, which we would provide in US$500,000 disbursements over three years.

As a sign of good faith, we purchased two more vehicles for donation to SAT. The original SUVs we had donated twelve years before were falling apart. I had known this for some time, so while Tony and Vincent were in Chicago, much to their amazement, we rushed off to the Toyota dealership. Tony and Vincent rapidly picked out a truck and an SUV. They were amazed and very grateful at how quickly I could make this decision and even more grateful that they could choose two vehicles that would best fit their needs. Again, this is the advantage of not having to run this decision through the board approval process.

With the loan, we could now expand the Rising Schools Program to an additional 470 schools, and once again 60 percent of these schools would be those we categorized as C and D schools.

This time our requirements for continuation of the loan included a minimum repayment rate by proprietors of 88 percent, a provision that loan interest rates must not exceed 25 percent in the first two years of the agreement, and an agreement that by the conclusion of the loan period with SAT, the program must provide training to at least 470 schools and disburse at least 423 loans. SAT calculated that the average loan size would be US$5,210 with an average term of eighteen months and a grace period of two months. So this was quite different from where we started with smaller loans and shorter terms.

We still had a long way to go before reaching full sustainability in our alliance with Sinapi Aba, but at least the possibility was now in sight.

BUILDING FUTURES:

A STORY OF ANOTHER SCHOOL PROPRIETOR

PAULINA NLANDO

Paulina's Queensland School (Accra, Ghana)

As I write these words in 2025, Paulina Nlando (whom we first met in the prologue) is still the proprietor of Paulina's Queensland School, located in the Agbogbloshie Market, Accra. When she started her school in 2003, it was one of three in the area. Now it is one of ten.

About forty thousand people live in the Agbogbloshie Market. Initially Paulina started in the market as a yam seller, but upon observing that a good number of the local children were running around unsupervised and were not attending school, she decided to take matters into her own hands. The children were vulnerable. Some had been kidnapped and held for ransom, some killed by the many vehicles that traverse the market, and others were lured into joining local gangs.

She knew that these children should be in school, but the local government school was too far away. She walked around the market collecting names of parents who might be interested in placing their children in a school with her, and when she realized that there was sufficient need and interest, she launched operations. Her beginnings were humble. With no formal structure to support the school, she brought her children together to teach them the alphabet, basic mathematics, and music. Starting with just ten girls and two boys, slowly but surely their number increased. When there became too many for her to manage, she hired high school graduates to assist her.

She decided to name the school Paulina's Queensland School because initially there were more girls enrolled than boys, but importantly, she believed that with a good education, all the little girls in her school could grow up to be "queens." The motto of the school is, "Where zeroes become heroes."

After connecting with Sinapi Aba and going through the Rising Schools Program, she learned through financial literacy training how to separate her school finances from her yam business. As of 2022, she was the proprietor of an impressive and well-attended institution. Her facilities included a computer lab and a well-stocked library. When the member of Parliament for her district visited and saw this, he observed that even most state schools weren't as well equipped. Paulina makes both the lab and the library available to the community and doesn't charge for usage.

Pre-COVID, the number of enrolled students stood at around 450. By the time the pandemic largely subsided in 2022, her enrollment was down to around 320 students. But, as of 2023, she is building attendance back up.

In 2024, fees were approximately GHS₵200 per term, equivalent to around US$13. Between twenty-five and thirty students are on scholarship at any given time. When parents have three children in the school, they are charged half price for the third child, and if they place four children in the school, one is educated free of charge.

When Paulina started her school, all the students came from within the market. Although this is still mostly the case, the school has started to draw students from the surrounding communities, in no small part because of the academic reputation of the school.

Paulina's main form of recruitment for new students comes from recommendations given by parents of children who attend the school. Paulina's Queensland School has never really had to market or advertise—a testament to the overall satisfaction of students and parents.

Many of the teachers also come from within the market, and as with student recruitment, the reputation of the school is a key element in attracting excellent teachers, often from further afield, to join the staff.

She tracks the progress of her students, many of whom have gone on to universities. Some are now lawyers, journalists, bankers, and engineers. Many former students return frequently to visit her. Teachers are very proud of the school and the number of students whose lives they have affected. They see many of their former students already taking on leadership roles in Ghana. And many teachers continue to further their own education while teaching at the school. One teacher relates that he came to the school as a teacher with nothing more than a high school education, but now he has completed a university degree. He credits the school as his inspiration and motivator and tells me that he is not the only teacher to further his education.

They have faced and continue to face multiple challenges given their location. The pollution present in the market is significant, and there is little they can do about it. Occasionally the school has lost students whose parents chose a better environment in which to live and raise their children.

The school received frequent visits from the Accra Metropolitan Assembly (AMA), which told Paulina that she needed to expand the spaces in which they were operating, particularly for the early childhood learners. The school was threatened with closure if it did not do so, so expansion became a priority. With some planning, the school was able to increase its footprint, and this satisfied the AMA.

Although the law requires that the government provide textbooks for private schools if the school is registered as a business and a school, the school must purchase its books from the market. Paulina and her staff would also like to see the government provide training, particularly when it comes to engaging in new curricula.

Paulina's teachers participated in the Sesame Workshop Techniques for Effective Teaching (TFET) course and spoke very highly of the experience. They particularly engaged with the modules around early childhood learning and those that concentrated on developing the interests of learners by using improvised and found materials as teaching tools. The workshop also prompted considerable adjustments in their disciplinary techniques. After exposure to the training, teachers relied less on negative interactions such as shouting and insulting students and understood that using the cane only results in disengagement and unhappiness. They have embraced the idea of making every learner feel like a part of the class.

The school now plays the videos to all teachers, including the nursery teachers, and those who attended TFET share what they learned with the rest of the faculty. This is typical for any kind of training program in which Queensland teachers participate. When a teacher returns from a training course, the teacher is invited to share everything they have learned with the full faculty at a scheduled meeting.

Paulina dreams of building another school, perhaps a boarding school and maybe even a secondary school. She takes enormous pride in the reputation of her school. It gives her great pleasure to learn that after they leave Queensland, her pupils are often singled out by the school they attend next and are asked where they received such fine primary education.

Her greatest satisfaction, however, is when a learner returns to tell them, "It is through Queensland I have been able to achieve my dreams and become the person I have become today."

PART III

CHANGE THAT LASTS

The first low-fee private school I ever saw in Ghana, Paulina's Queensland School (aka The Queensland Primary School), as it looked in 2008 when I first met its owner, Paulina Nlando.

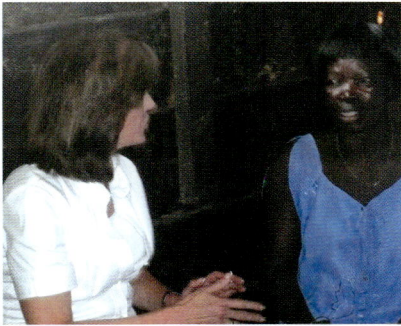

The meeting that started it all—me listening to Paulina tell her story of running her school in the Agbogbloshie Market.

Inside Paulina's school, 2008.

A child sits in the market among yam sellers.

Yam porters at the Agbogbloshie Market. Many have babies strapped on their backs.

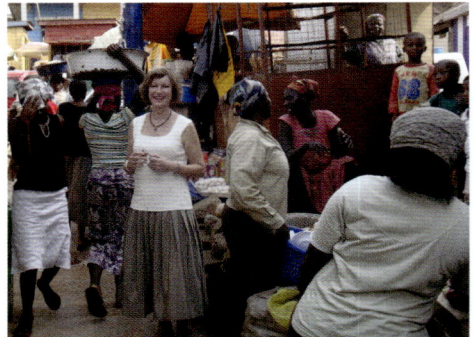

Walking through the vibrant Agbogbloshie Market in Accra.

Liesel and I traveled across Ghana to gain a deeper understanding of the low-fee private school landscape. It was challenging work, but we also had a lot of fun!

Tony Fosu and I early on in our partnership with Sinapi Aba.

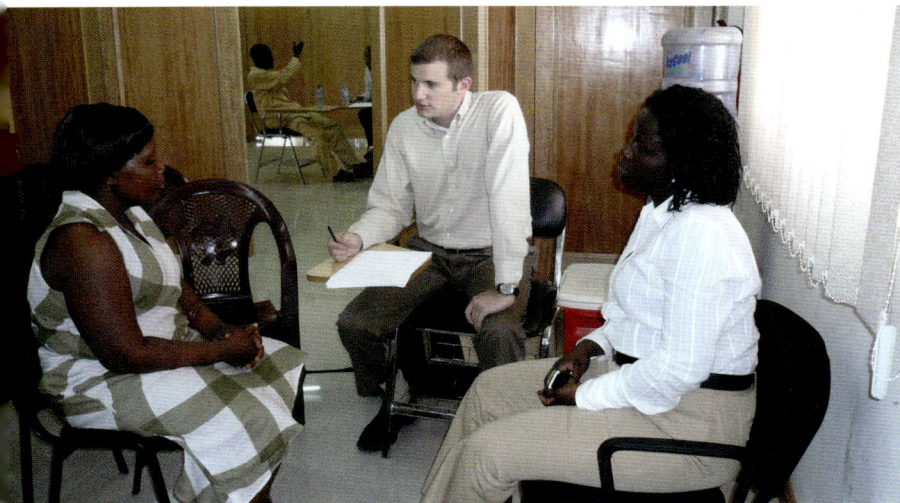

Andy Sprunger administers a proprietor questionnaire in 2008.

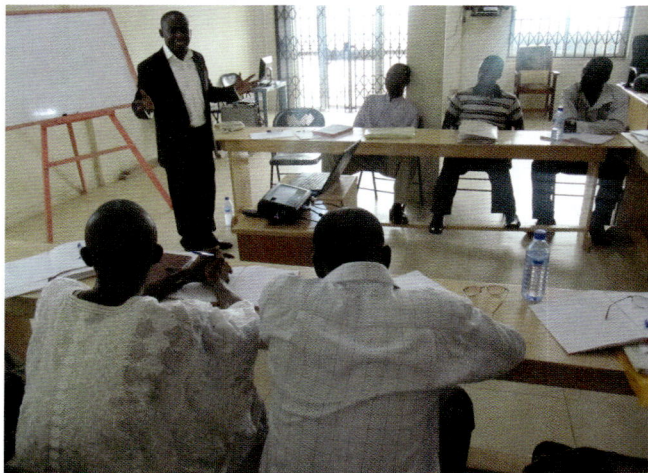

Vincent Amponsah, head of business at Sinapi Aba, conducts proprietor training.

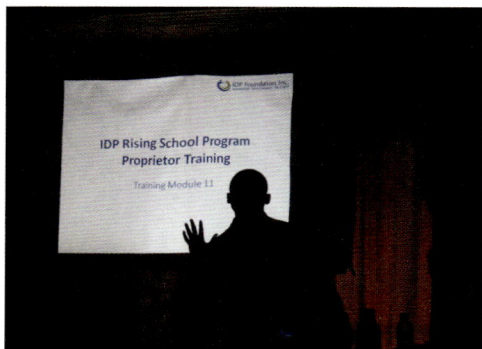

Proprietor training is an essential pillar of the Rising Schools Program (RSP).

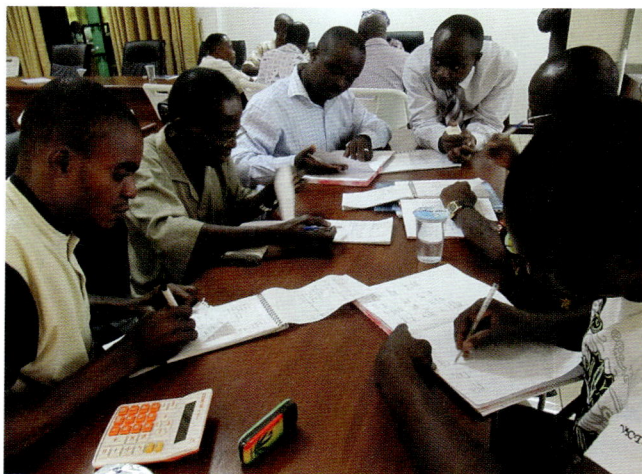

Proprietors at work during the RSP trainings.

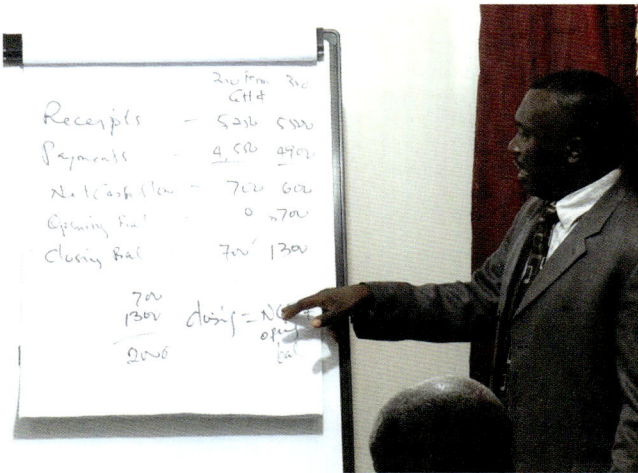

A Sinapi Aba loan officer trains proprietors.

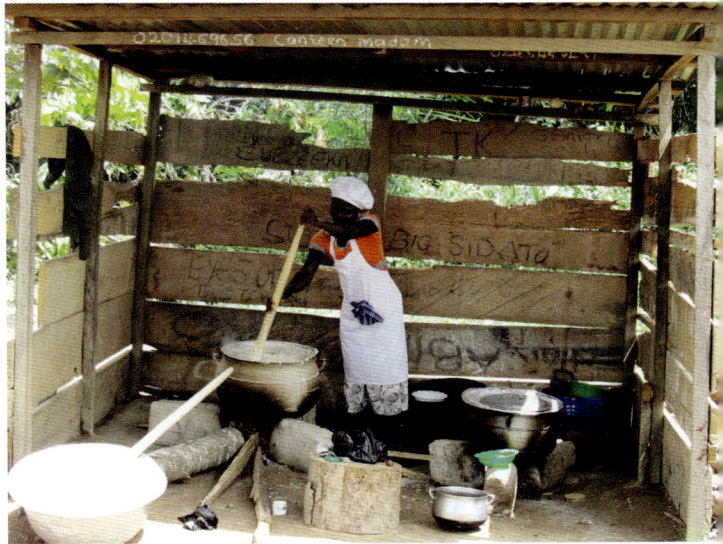

During catering training, school owners learned proper hygiene and safety measures to use in their kitchens.

School caterers smile with pride in their new aprons and chef's hats.

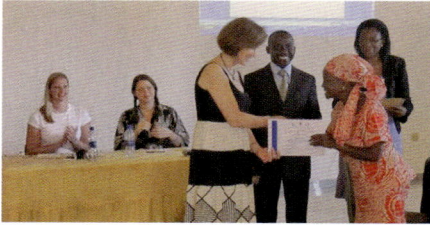
Presenting a certificate of completion to a proprietor in recognition of successfully completing the RSP proprietor training program.

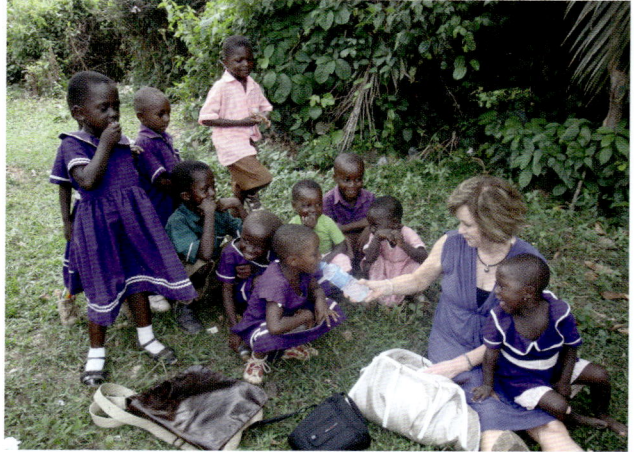
A school visit in 2009.

All the schools I visited early on had minimal infrastructure.

A rural low-fee private school outside of Kumasi, Ghana.

In this school, the classrooms were separated by blackboards, making it exceptionally noisy and hard to concentrate.

This little girl couldn't attend the school due to the fees, so she stood outside looking in. Her story is told in chapter 3.

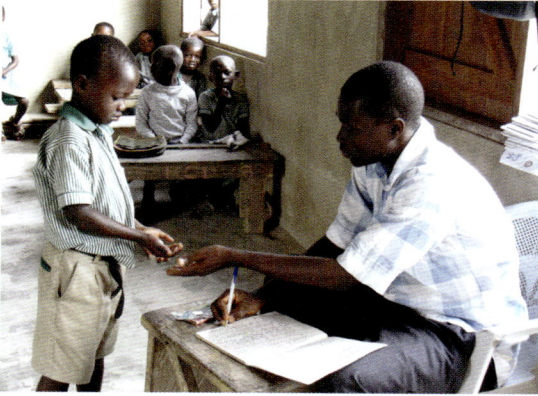

A proprietor at his low-fee private school collecting fees.

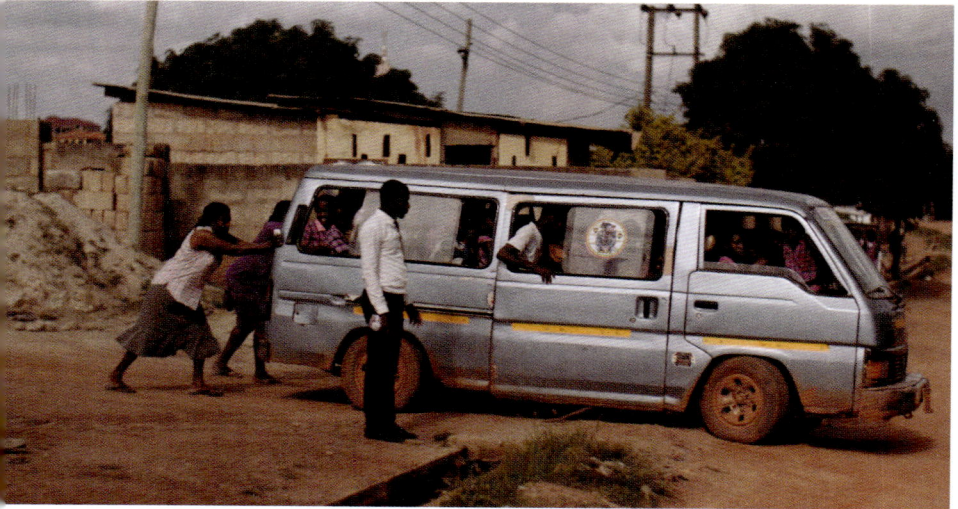

A very full school bus. Many loans were used to purchase school buses.

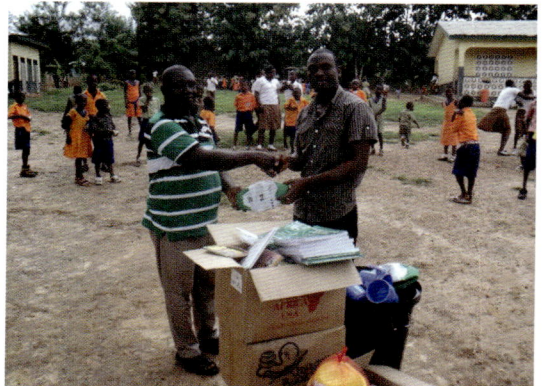

Raphael Akomeah of the Sinapi Aba/IDPF team delivers donated supplies to a school in 2012, a story that is told in chapter 4.

Sesame Workshop Muppeteers during the filming of the Techniques for Effective Teaching (TFET) video series.

TFET video filming.

Groups participate in TFET training.

Students use TFET techniques.

Stephen Adu, director of basic education for the Ghana Education Service (GES), delivers the opening address of the 2012 Education Stakeholders' Conference. The topic was public–private partnerships, as outlined in chapter 6.

From left: Ernest Dzandu, me, Christian Koramoah, Stephen Adu, and Rachel Hinton at the Education Stakeholders' Conference in 2012 in Ghana.

Over the years since the program began, I made numerous trips to Ghana. Here I am with Paulina— reconnecting with the woman who inspired me so deeply.

School proprietor Paa Willie.

Paa Willie's school under construction with funds from an RSP loan.

Pa Willie's school after an RSP infrastructure loan to add a concrete floor and a safety enclosure for students.

Lily Baah at her school in 2012 during construction utilizing RSP loans.

Lily Baah's fully renovated school, made possible through multiple RSP loans.

Our amazing driver Charles Adjei-Boateng, with his daughter, Pritzka (named in my honor), alongside school proprietor Lily Baah.

Magdalene Sackey's Phiga School before an RSP loan.

Phiga School during construction with RSP loans which included a land purchase.

Phiga School after RSP loans.

In January 2021, schools were allowed to reopen following the COVID-19 outbreak if students wore protective face coverings.

Me speaking at a panel at Forbes Summit on Philanthropy.

I've also spoken at the UNESCO Education for All Global Monitoring Report Launch (as seen here), the United Nations Global Conference on Social Change, the Sabanci Foundation on Philanthropy for Education, and many more.

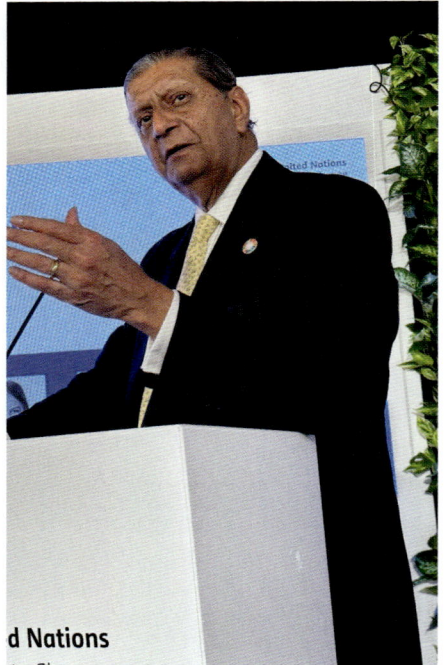

Amir Dossal, the former executive director of the United Nations Office for Partnerships, who would turn out to become one of my greatest supporters and facilitators.

The IDP Foundation team retreat in 2022.

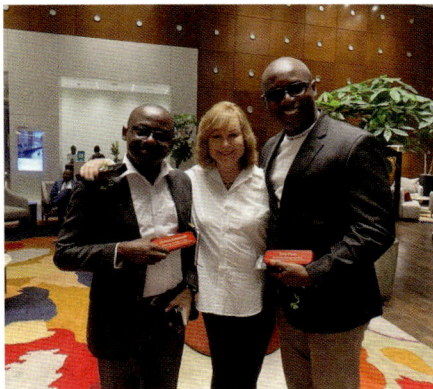

With Tony Fosu and Vincent Amponsah from Sinapi Aba.

With four RSP alumni at our fifteenth anniversary celebration in Accra in 2024.

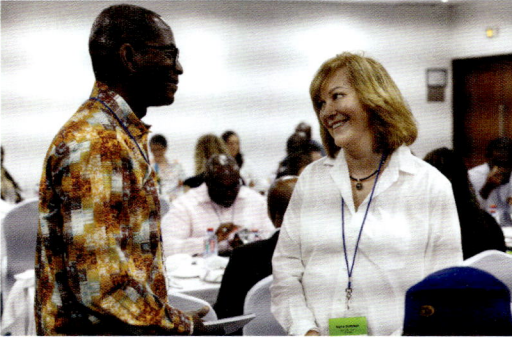

With Patrick Awuah, president of Ashesi University, at our partners dinner in Ghana in 2024.

With Professor Damasus Tuurosong, president of the Ghana National Association of Private Schools.

Paulina Nlando.

As of 2025, Paulina continues to run her school in the market and has made many improvements, including permanent concrete structures and more classrooms. When she started the school it only went through grade three. It now goes all the way through junior high.

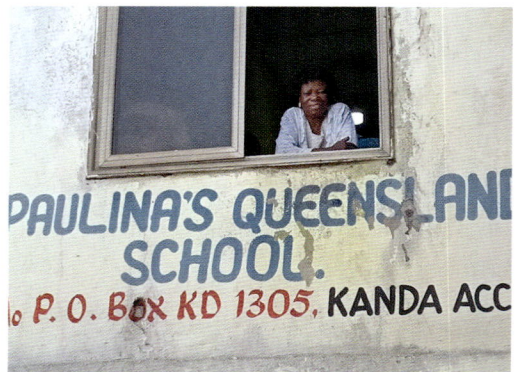

Chapter 8

IMPACT INVESTING

In 2011, Liesel challenged me with a question that would change the way I thought about philanthropy and investment. She was full of challenges, that girl!

"So, you're on your way to figuring out how to help school proprietors be creditworthy and included in the lending practices of microfinance institutions like Sinapi Aba. Amazing!" she said.

"Yes. We're onto something here," I said, noticing that she had a distinct tone in her voice, a tone that implied an agenda. I looked at her suspiciously.

She continued, "Well, these microfinance institutions are connected to larger investment vehicles that access debt from the capital markets. If we believe organizations like Sinapi Aba are worthy of our grant capital, shouldn't we also consider where the rest of our foundation's investments are going?"

Her argument was simple but powerful.

That conversation set me on a path I hadn't anticipated—one that would lead the IDP Foundation to embrace a new way of investing, aligning financial returns with our mission to create lasting change. In 2011, this approach had a name: *impact investing.*

The term was relatively new. In fact, the whole idea of investing to enact actual positive change in the world only started to emerge comprehensively around 2006. As investors were trying to figure out what to call the practice, the issue ended up dominating many conferences. The real problem was that there simply weren't that many institutional-quality managers who had the training to deliver decent market returns from investments that also had a positive impact on social and environmental causes.

In response, a new group of professionals developed. These impact managers, often called environmental, social, and governance (ESG) managers, select companies with portfolios that achieve these dual goals.

Ordinarily, when wealth advisors evaluate potential managers on behalf of their clients, they ask questions like, *Do they have a consistent track record? Has the team worked together for a long time? Can they navigate different market environments? Do they have style drift and frequently change the sectors or instruments they invest in, or can they remain focused?*

In the early discussions around impact, there were many managers who fulfilled all the necessary financial functions but not many who understood how to do well financially while also aiding social and environmental causes. There were some early pioneers, of course, but not many, and with the scarcity of such managers practicing then, it was difficult for investors interested in ESG to build a complete portfolio.

As you might imagine, the idea was generally dismissed by traditional wealth managers who didn't understand the concept and cautioned clients that a focus on impact would result in diminished and concessionary returns.

> The choice of investment is not an either/or choice. You can achieve more than adequate returns and do good at the same time.

When we introduced the idea to our wealth advisors, they were as confused and concerned as I had been. Liesel deserves the credit for bringing impact investing to the IDP Foundation, which was crucially important to her in her own investment portfolios. She was way ahead of the curve and was a trailblazer in the impact investing world.

As our debate around impact investing continued, Liesel encouraged our advisors to do some research and go to conferences. She ended up schooling both me and our wealth advisors. Eventually, the choice of investment is not an either/or choice. You can achieve more than adequate returns and do good at the same time. I joined her in the call to action.

Slowly but surely, our advisors also learned enough to piece the narrative together. Once they started, the idea snowballed. Today they invest 85 percent of their clients' assets in ways that are mission-aligned. It has become a core competency for their practice, and if you don't mind me bragging a bit, they give Liesel and me full credit for starting them down this path at such an early stage. They are now recognized leaders in this field and have a significant role on the speaking circuit, explaining and promoting impact investments to the industry.

We made investments in organizations, companies, enterprises, and funds with the intention of not only generating an above-market financial return but also having a positive social and environmental return.

It is important at this stage to note that there is, in fact, a whole continuum in the way organizations approach impact investing. Every organization develops its own criteria. Some organizations will simply negative screen. They research, identify, and then exclude the stocks of companies whose operations are to one degree or another harmful because of their ESG practices. When those practices conflict with the mission of your organization, you remove them from your portfolio.

But it's equally important to actively embrace ESG managers and strategies that are consistent with your mission. Our wealth advisors, in addition to negatively screening out the companies that conflict with our values, recommend managers whose actions are consistent with our mission in the public markets. Furthermore, they work closely with our investment committee, which is responsible for building out the private market allocation of our portfolio.

Impact investing can be executed in two ways. You can move toward market-rate financial returns in concert with a very strong impact. But some organizations prefer to put impact at the forefront and are willing to accept less than market returns, or concessionary returns, if the impact thesis is strong enough.

At IDPF, we are currently invested across the whole universe of equities. Getting to that point has been a long journey with lessons learned all along the way—work that was well worth the effort. With the help of our advisors, we have designed a custom report to measure impact and scrutinize our holdings. I'm proud to say that our investment program is nearly 100 percent mission-aligned and impact invested.

Wealth advisors don't manage any of the money themselves. Their primary role is education, helping clients to determine the right asset allocation and finding appropriate third-party managers and strategies to build an effective mission-aligned investment program. As impact investing has gained popularity, a lot of people have jumped on the bandwagon, making it even more important to have a partner at the table who understands what's real and what isn't. Now that it's gone mainstream, and everybody wants to do it, there are both pretenders and real engagers. I would advise anyone going down this path to research whether their advisors and managers delivered in the past and, more importantly, whether they can deliver moving forward.

The most important force in creating greater recognition for impact investing has been the younger investor. They are a huge consumer group demanding a change in the approach of investment houses and have been very effective in communicating this movement to the rest of the world. We know that younger people tend to be more interested in fair labor practices and supply chains and are twice as likely to check product packaging to make sure that it is environmentally friendly and sustainably sourced. As investors, they look for companies that are not only profitable but also responsible when it comes to the planet and human rights.

And while the movement is not solely the province of young investors, they have proven to be huge drivers of change, partly due to their use of all forms of social media to promote their position loudly and often.

Now that more clients are starting to demand impact investing, there is more pressure on analysts to start really investigating impact funds to make sure that they aren't just calling themselves an impact fund but that their actions support their claims. And now that impact investing has become a mainstream choice rather than merely a boutique idea, the larger investment houses are being pushed to consider impact funds. Even if the shift toward ESG investing is not going as fast as we would like, it is certainly moving in the right direction.

SUSTAINABLE DEVELOPMENT GOALS

As previously mentioned, the Sustainable Development Goals (SDGs) are seventeen global objectives adopted by the United Nations in 2015 to eradicate poverty, protect the planet, and build a peaceful and prosperous world. They replaced the original eight Millennium Development Goals (MDGs) established in 2000 that were failing to reach their targets.

The seventeen SDGs consist of 169 targets that lay out universal action items addressing the most important global challenges, which include poverty, hunger, health, education, global warming, and gender equality. The aim is to achieve these goals by 2030. (For further details on the SDGs, see Appendix A.)

In early 2017, we incorporated alignment with the SDGs into our impact investment practices. It is an important part of what we do, the underlying thread that binds all our philanthropic activities. Today, we proactively gather data from individual fund impact reports and fund managers to create a profile that systematically measures each impact fund according to the SDGs.

We have been tracking our portfolio's performance against existing benchmarks since 2014, and our performance has always outperformed those benchmarks. It's encouraging and rewarding to see these types of results. My daughter was right, once again.

BRIDGING THE GAP BETWEEN GRANTS AND INVESTMENTS

At the IDP Foundation, we use a variety of tools to provide catalytic capital to achieve impact. One tool is program-related investments (PRIs), which are often overlooked by grant-making foundations. PRIs can provide catalytic philanthropic capital to social entrepreneurs. I believe more foundations would be willing to use them if they understood them better.

Before PRIs came into being through a tax reform act in 1969, foundations were encumbered by the Prudent Investor Rule, whereby foundation money could not be subject to "unnecessary" risk. This effectively prevented philanthropic investments in fledgling, mission-oriented ventures. After 1969, high-risk investments qualified as philanthropy, so long as they significantly advanced a foundation's charitable intent.

The use of PRIs is restricted to grant-making foundations, which allows us to make use of them. Through PRIs we can make risky investments in the form of debt or equity or some form of blended finance with the potential for high returns in terms of social impact. Sometimes we make an investment in US dollars, and sometimes we assume currency risk. We structure things in all sorts of ways. This includes PRIs.

PRIs are bridges between grant-making and investment opportunities. If the PRI is a debt investment, upon return of the principal at the end of the loan period, the principal can be plowed back into the corpus of the foundation; if the PRI is an equity investment, then when the foundation sells its shares or ownership stake in the company, the proceeds—consisting of the original investment (return of capital) plus any profit—can be reinvested into the foundation's corpus. However, interest or profit earned on PRIs is subject to the excise tax on net investment income. And if the debt or equity investment fails, then that investment can be written off as a grant. However, in giving away 5 percent of the value of the foundation annually, as mandated by law, all program-related expenses count toward that 5 percent. So as long as 5 percent goes out the door in the form of grants, program-related investments, or program-related expenses, all is fine.

The contracts for all PRIs that the foundation makes state clearly that the purpose of the investment is in significant furtherance of our charitable purpose and that we require reporting that includes impact reporting. Sometimes it makes very good sense for a foundation to provide early money in either debt or equity investments instead of grants to help projects get off the ground. I would like to share three examples that have very inspiring and interesting stories.

1. MORINGA CONNECT

To tell the story of Moringa Connect, I also must tell the story of our engagement with the Harambeans. In 2017, we had one of our project managers investigate how we might connect the foundation with African social enterprise organizations other than the schools in the Rising Schools Program.

We were invested in several social impact funds, and I was becoming increasingly interested in the types of companies within those funds. This led us to meet with Yasmin Kumi, who had recently started volunteering for an organization called Harambeans while simultaneously forming her own consulting company called The African Foresight Group (AFG).

Harambeans was founded by Okendo Lewis-Gayle in 2008. Born in Costa Rica and raised in Italy, he eventually made his way to Harvard's Kennedy School, where he developed his vision of starting a networking alliance for African-born entrepreneurs. Harambe, which means "working toward a common purpose" in Swahili, was his solution for addressing the African continent's ubiquitous economic challenges. He believes, as I also believe, that aid is an unsustainable solution.

Harambeans quickly became an impressive network for African innovators running social enterprises that were creating positive and scalable change in their communities. Participants were all highly educated individuals, many of whom had attended prestigious Western academic institutions, with a passion to return to their native countries to start businesses that could address pressing social or economic needs. The alliance provided them with essential resources, such as access to training, markets, capital, and support networks.

I was deeply impressed with both Yasmin and Okendo. Though Harambeans was about ten years old, it hadn't yet attracted significant financial investment. It was time they had a pioneering commitment to help them grow.

Yasmin explained that there were entrepreneurs like her at different stages in their development at Harambeans. Some were very advanced. Some were very young or early in their careers. Some were somewhere in the middle. "We try to build different pathways for different types of entrepreneurs in the alliance that are funded by different partners," she shared.

I wanted to partner with Harambeans to support social enterprises that had already raised funds or had some revenue but were having trouble finding more partners and funders. In keeping with the philosophy of the foundation, I wanted to help their businesses scale successfully.

Over a series of discussions, we decided to create and fund together the Global Access Program (GAP), a yearlong program designed to support five Harambean entrepreneurs across five key areas: capital, talent, strategic partnerships, exposure to investors, and leadership.

Our first cohort of GAP fellows, in 2018, included Kwami Williams of Moringa Connect, Ugwem Eneyo of Shyft Power Solutions, Obinna Okwodu of Fibre, Margaret Nyamumbo of Kahawa 1893, and Adetayo Bamiduro of Max.ng. By the end of their year, our inaugural class was able to raise more than US$8.2 million, hire over one hundred people, and increase revenues in their enterprises by more than 40 percent. Today, these high-impact businesses continue to thrive and are extremely successful.

Moringa Connect (doing business as True Moringa), founded by Kwami Williams, who was born and raised in Accra, really caught my attention. Kwami had been studying aerospace engineering at MIT and had started to live his lifelong dream of working at NASA by interning at two space centers. However, during his time at university, he returned to Ghana on a class trip in 2012, and upon seeing the level of poverty in rural regions, he decided that he needed to do whatever he could to address the situation. He was particularly taken with the plight of moringa tree farmers.

Various non-governmental organizations (NGOs) and aid agencies had been funding rural farmers to grow moringa trees because of their remarkable properties and their lucrative potential. The leaves have high levels of vitamin A, have more iron than spinach, are richer in protein than yogurt, and contain more calcium than milk. And their seeds contain a nourishing oil that is also deeply moisturizing. The trees, which do well in arid climates and need very little water, are twenty times more effective at capturing and removing CO^2 than general vegetation.

The farmers were told that when the trees matured, the agencies would buy their leaves and seeds. However, financial aid eventually dried up, and there had been no effort to help the farmers develop a market for their crops. With little to no economic benefit from their efforts and a significant amount of moringa leaves from the now mature moringa trees, the farmers were at a loss as to what to do.

While visiting these farms, Kwami met Emily Cunningham, who had been studying development economics at Harvard. The two decided to form a partnership. They took the seeds back to MIT and studied how to cold-press them for oil. They discovered that the resulting oil outperformed jojoba, shea, and argan oils. Starting in 2014, Kwami and Emily developed a network of around five thousand farmers who collectively have planted three million moringa trees, generating rural incomes, improving nutrition for farmers, and afforesting rural areas.

Unfortunately, in 2019 they experienced devastating farm and factory fires that threatened the viability of their entire business, losing close to US$1 million in assets and revenue. Rather than give up, they doubled down on their mission, took all necessary measures to be resilient, and quickly turned things around. Kwami had initially converted his parents' home into a processing plant, but now that the business had scaled, he began using a commercial warehouse in Nsawam, Ghana, and the company created seventy nonfarm jobs along its supply chain.

I was deeply impressed with the scope, passion, and vision Kwami had for his company. He had managed to lift rural farmers, especially women, out of poverty while operating a potentially highly profitable company manufacturing very desirable and healthful products. Seventy-five percent of the farmers he engaged were among the poorest 20 percent of the Ghanaian population.

He was seeking capital to support his operations and his marketing and advertising strategies. He wanted to support the construction of a world-class factory powered by organic, renewable energy; offer long-term loans and financial literacy programs to farmers; and help them improve their knowledge of agronomy. His ambitions aligned significantly with six of the seventeen SDGs: (1) no poverty, (2) zero hunger, (3) good health and well-being, (5) gender equality, (13) climate action, and (15) life on land.

In April 2021, we decided to make a US$150,000 PRI debt investment into Moringa Connect. The primary purpose of the PRI was not to produce income, as it was risky, but rather to further the mission and impact of both our organizations.

In 2023, we made a US$150,000 working capital bridge loan PRI to Moringa Connect to ensure that while they were raising larger debt from other financial institutions, they would have the capital to fuel their current traction and ensure that they were able to continue making timely investments in farm expansion, raw material purchases from farmers, and manufacturing runs for existing and new products.

They are currently manufacturing moringa-powered herbal tea, a nutritional supplement, and skincare products under their award-winning brand, True Moringa. They have also built partnerships with Whole Foods, Macy's, and the Home Shopping Network, among other retail outlets. Meanwhile, True Moringa field officers work directly with their farmers to provide guidance on how to maximize crop yields and offer training in financial literacy.

This has turned unbanked farmers into active participants in Village Savings and Loan Associations (VSLAs). Their model enables farmers to increase their incomes by two to five times.

The company has never missed a loan repayment to us and continues to grow at a remarkable rate. They also provide scholarships for farmers and their family members to pursue higher education. They provide clean drinking water to seven hundred people in the Basabasa community and have raised funds to repair wells in five surrounding communities. They have also renovated and outfitted rural hospitals with lifesaving medical equipment, demonstrating a truly holistic approach to community development, climate impact, and improving rural farmer livelihoods.

2. AKO ADJEI PARK IN ACCRA

Will Senyo is the CEO and cofounder of Ako Adjei Park Ltd., Ghana. He had a vision for developing a small-business enclave for young innovators and social entrepreneurs. The idea was to design a mixed-use distributed campus of live-work-play spaces targeting three core communities: tech entrepreneurs, social entrepreneurs, and creatives from Ghana's bustling art scene.

Will wanted to attract founders of companies focused on a variety of emerging sectors, such as agriculture, healthcare, finance, and education. Many of the young founders he was targeting were making progress creating new business models at the intersection of technology and social impact. However, they were encountering significant challenges. They needed reliable access to power, internet access, and office space but couldn't afford the two years of rent generally required up front by most landlords in Ghana. Will envisioned renovating a cluster of buildings in a vibrant oceanfront neighborhood just east of Accra's central business district to provide offices and plug-and-play spaces for coworking, hosting conferences, networking events, and incubation and acceleration programs. The entire project was designed to be driven by principles of sustainability, including the use of solar energy to power the building.

Before he came to the IDP Foundation, Will was finding it difficult to secure money. When he approached Ghanaian financiers, they only wanted to hear about proven and already profitable concepts. His pleas fell on deaf ears, and he couldn't get funding to get the project started. Knowing that our foundation was active in Ghana, he came to us with a proposal requesting a debt investment.

"If you will step up and be our anchor funder," he said, "then others will come." But upon review, I felt that I needed a consultant to conduct due diligence on his business plan and projections before committing.

By then, Yasmin Kumi's consulting company, African Foresight Group (AFG), was fully operative. This seemed like a perfect opportunity to employ her considerable gifts to look at Will's proposal. We paid for AFG's consultancy and shared the results with Will. Sharing due diligence results with a potential investment recipient is uncommon, but we wanted him to succeed. AFG's recommendations led to key revisions, and Will adjusted his projections and business plan. Ultimately, we made a US$350,000 PRI debt investment. Will achieved his expansion. The project is profitable and continues to grow, with people clamoring for desk space. Now other investors are coming out of the woodwork to support him, and he is continuing to expand his campus, purchasing land and starting new construction. He has also been careful to collaborate with community leaders to ensure that the project is acceptable to the local population.

We also continued to expand and in 2020 moved our offices into Ako Adjei Park, which turned out to be a win-win for everybody.

At the IDP Foundation, we're not afraid of risk. We've been particularly successful in supporting socially responsible, revenue-generating companies that have been able to achieve self-sufficiency. We have been able to do it by introducing business due diligence and financial rigor to those projects. The worst approach would have been simply handing over grant funding to establish his business. Due diligence wasn't just about assessing risk and opportunity for us as investors—it was a critical learning experience for him as an entrepreneur. Through the process, he had to refine his thinking, adjust his projections, and demonstrate his ability to manage debt responsibly. This discipline was essential to setting him on a sustainable path. Our collaboration with him is a prime example of how philanthropic dollars can be used for impact investing—not just providing capital but also building long-term capacity.

Today, Will's vision of creating a fifteen-building live-work-play innovation enclave in the heart of Accra is coming to fruition. He has created a center where experimentation toward establishing a sustainable and inclusive city is being brought to life. As Will likes to say, "Ako Adjei Park is the living, breathing social lab of Accra." Ako Adjei Park's developed spaces have even played host to world leaders, such as French President Emmanuel Macron, former Dutch Prime Minister Mark Rutte, and former German Chancellor Angela Merkel. They all visited to engage with the young Ghanaians who are building an alternative future for themselves and their country.

In mid-2023, we made another US$250,000 PRI loan to enable Ako Adjei to support workspaces for small- and medium-sized enterprises (SMEs) with the intention of leading to program sustainability within the operations of Ako Adjei. The loan fits perfectly into the IDP Foundation's mission by developing SMEs in an economically disadvantaged community to create jobs for underserved individuals and to empower and develop the local economy and lift community members out of poverty.

3. EDOVO

Edovo first came to our attention through our investment in Impact Engine, a Chicago-based startup accelerator focused on businesses that deliver both strong financial returns and positive social impact. The IDP Foundation participated in Impact Engine's first fund, and a few years later, we were offered a co-investment opportunity in one of their portfolio companies: Edovo.

Founded by Brian Hill in 2013, Edovo is a Chicago-based organization whose mission is to help those adversely affected by incarceration build better lives for themselves. The company first did so by providing tablets and wireless networks designed specifically for correctional facilities to deliver digital educational programming.

Each year, more than ten million Americans cycle through jail, and more than US$80 billion is spent on incarceration. The recidivism rate is disgraceful—greater than 50 percent. Edovo hopes to address this problem by making quality access to education and opportunity a reality for all. Edovo discovered that it could reduce the 50 percent recidivism rate to as low as 43 percent through educational programs in prisons.

However, correctional facilities usually lack the resources and funding to provide educational programming to their populations. This can lead to increased incidences of violence and a failure to adequately prepare those who are released from prison to reenter society.

Edovo started by providing its own tablets and became a provider of uniform educational software for use across every major tablet or any other connected computing device. Today there are over one million tablets inside correctional facilities. On the Edovo platform, each learner has a personal account and can begin or continue their coursework by logging in on any device, even after they have been released from prison.

Edovo's platform is centered around educational attainment and self-improvement, with curricula like GED preparation and for-credit, post-secondary-school courses. In addition to education, tablets also offer access to cognitive behavioral therapy (CBT) and vocational and life-skills training. Some facilities use a reward system where credits for entertainment serve as incentives for sustained engagement and the achievement of educational goals. The educational tools on each tablet are self-directed and goal-driven, which allows learners to go at their own pace and pursue their interests in a highly personalized manner. Edovo also offers preparation for nationally recognized job certifications and provides social–emotional learning (SEL) tools to address anger management, substance abuse, and parenting while incarcerated.

One of the most effective uses of the Edovo platform has been in enabling incarcerated individuals to take a record of their accomplishments on the tablet for use in court at probation and parole hearings. Producing better outcomes at these hearings has been a remarkably effective tool for reducing prison sentences.

Now that tablets are becoming ubiquitous within the system, Edovo believes it should be possible to reach nearly 100 percent of the incarcerated population within a few years, which could make an enormous difference: Edovo discovered that 10 to 20 percent of the prison population could be released and go home immediately using existing legislation and earned time credit laws if only they had access to Edovo's programming.

Parole boards and judges scrutinize prisoners' claims that they have been engaging in productive activities. In institutions without tablets, options for prisoners to substantiate their claims are limited, but after engaging on the Edovo platform, prisoners can present tangible, quantifiable demonstrations of their activities. They can point to the courses they've completed, the grades they've received, and the number of days they've spent in the program. Edovo provides an opportunity for prisoners to demonstrate a willingness to engage with the world productively and improve themselves. The actual improvement was apparent: jails and prisons saw significant decreases in violent incidents after Edovo tablets launched across the facilities.

Additionally, there are often expensive programs that need to be completed during probation or parole, including substance abuse courses. This post-release burden can now be lightened as they can complete courses prior to release or afterward through the EdovoGO platform.

Edovo curates, creates, and licenses content on the platform. They have partnered with, among others, organizations like the American Suicide Prevention Association, Grow with Google, MasterClass, and the Lionheart Foundation.

For the first three years of operation, the staff of Edovo spent most of their energy convincing the market that tablets could exist and function in prisons. There were, of course, many questions from correctional institutions about safety and security. After managing to convince the facilities with which they hoped to engage that the program was sound, the next question concerned capital: Who was going to pay for the tablets?

The infrastructure and wireless networks needed to run the program would require a substantial investment. The answer seemed to lie in engaging with prison phone companies. However, given the well-known and significant pricing abuses by those companies—who were taking advantage of a captive prison population—Edovo purchased a phone company to disrupt that narrative and scale its educational tablet operation.

Within three years, Edovo concluded that it would never have more than a portion of the market, meaning that the reach of Edovo's self-improvement platform would be limited. They were spending far too much time running the phone company, which was eating into Edovo's effort to expand the educational opportunities of its platform.

Edovo had succeeded in shifting the needle when it came to pricing by taking some large contracts from the major providers, but it faced headwinds from turning all its data over to regulators and being transparent about its operations with advocacy groups.

Gradually, other phone companies started adopting Edovo's language and policies, and because of their scale, they were able to provide lower call charges. Throughout this period, Brian met with competitors and encouraged them to rethink their models. This, in addition to the tremendous amount of external pressure exerted on the companies by social justice organizations and the market, finally resulted in shifts in policy toward more equitable business practices.

Having played a role in enacting the change they wanted to see, Edovo stepped out of the phone market. To effectively scale its educational impact and reach as many people as possible, it needs to partner and not compete. Once other phone companies began providing tablets themselves, reaching everyone meant being on every platform.

Edovo has been remarkably successful in extending its reach. It has partnered with every major provider and already scaled to almost forty of the fifty states, working with hundreds of facilities ranging from small county jails to statewide departments of correction. Edovo has seen close to 80 percent of weekly engagement levels from individuals with access to the platform. In 2016, Edovo was honored with the Global EdTech Startup Award given by the organizers of the world's largest edtech startup competition.

Edovo also has achieved a GIIRS Platinum rating. GIIRS stands for Global Impact Investing Rating System, which is "a comprehensive and transparent system for assessing the social and environmental impact of developed and emerging market companies and funds with a ratings and analytics approach." By the end of 2021, Edovo had approximately 35,000 tablets in the system. A year later that number had grown to 121,000; by April 2023 it was 210,000. Brian Hill believes that within the next two years he could reach over 50 percent of the incarcerated population.

In mid-2018, the IDP Foundation provided a PRI in the form of a high-risk equity position in Edovo. The investment aligned with our mission to support innovative, scalable, and sustainable solutions to seemingly insurmountable problems. Later that year we provided a US$750,000 debt PRI to provide Edovo with enough cash flow to install the tablets in another correctional institution.

Brian told me that both investments were critical to the success of his company:

> When you get an equity program-related investment (PRI), it becomes very important to protect the mission, because PRI investors can quickly rip out their investment if we go off mission, which is a strong incentive to stay on mission. PRI investment provides a very clear signaling mechanism that both encourages good investors and deters investors that may not actually be impact investors.
>
> When it comes to philanthropic debt investing, it's purely essential. The reality was that no one would lend us money. We were too young as a company. Standard terms were aggressively unfavorable and untenable. So really the only way in which we could meaningfully scale and drive the impact that we wanted was through PRI debt investment. The IDP Foundation and a handful of others were the only lenders at the table.
>
> The debt that the IDP Foundation provided was critical to our ability to even function as a company. Absent that, we would not have been able to launch Cook County (Chicago). We would not have been able to launch Kentucky. We would not have been able to launch Minnesota. It was not financially possible unless we raised further equity financing, which was also untenable and would have compounded challenges in the future.

Edovo paid off the debt before it was due.

Despite its continued outsized success in impact, there is still considerable apathy and lack of urgency within corrections that limit investments serving the incarcerated population, making long-term profitability elusive. Taking early financial returns and weighing the balance of limited profitability and exits that wouldn't jeopardize impact in the future, Edovo made the decision to return capital and pursue its scaled mission as a sustainable nonprofit. In this way, Edovo will continue to invest, rather than disinvest, in impact.

Edovo makes money by inducing governments to purchase a system that is powerful, scalable, and an efficient way to supplement in-person programming and meaningfully serve the incarcerated population.

It is exhilarating to invest in an organization that has the vision to take on an issue that is usually ignored. It is even more exciting to see them succeed in so many ways while creating systemic change and long-lasting impact. We are excited to follow Edovo's continued growth in the future.

OUR MISSION

As I look back on our earliest ventures in 2008 and explore the full spectrum of the foundation's activities since inception, I believe that we have developed a consistent philosophy. Our mission statement articulates that we are "dedicated to encouraging and supporting the development of innovative and sustainable solutions to complex global issues. Specifically, we support local and international partners who innovate, develop, and see progress in all forms of learning, from critical medical research to classroom education."

Although our key initiative is the Rising Schools Program, we have cultivated several philanthropic engagements with the medical research community, along with other catalytic granting and investment initiatives. These, combined with our development of a robust impact investment and program-related investment strategy, have given us cohesion.

As we entered 2019, however, I was asking myself many questions. I had started to think about the future of the foundation. Not the immediate future—I was very proud of the team we had built and our many accomplishments together—but the distant future. And I realized that for this family foundation to continue, ideally in perpetuity, I was going to have to start thinking about developing a long-term succession strategy.

Chapter 9

CHANGE IN THE AIR

The year 2019 brought significant change for both me and the IDP Foundation.

It began with a project to update the foundation's website. So much had evolved in recent years that the site no longer fully captured the scope of our work. As I worked through the updates, I realized we needed more than just refreshed content—we needed a short film that would serve as a call to action, inspiring others to follow our lead or partner with us to expand the program into new markets.

By coincidence, I received an email with an attached video from a fund manager who knew about our interest in impact investing and was hoping we would invest in his fund. Part of his pitch was asking for feedback on two short films about his work. They were both amazing.

I contacted him and asked how to get in touch with the filmmaker.

"You need to speak to Sham Sandhu," he said.

"Who's Sham Sandhu?" I asked.

"Well, Sham selected the filmmaker," he responded. "He was reviewing our organization as a whole, and he suggested that a film would be a great marketing tool and then helped me decide what kind of film to make. Then he helped us select the filmmaker."

He introduced me to Sham. Sham is a senior business advisor who specializes in leadership and team development. He works with leadership teams at global venture capital firms, family offices, and foundations that are focused on creating positive social, systemic, or environmental impact.

"These films were made by Jonathan Olinger," he told me. "He has a company called HUMAN." HUMAN is a world-leading storytelling agency and creative collective for international brands and social impact initiatives that want to reach a global audience through media.

I went to Jonathan's website and was blown away by the quality of his films and his list of impressive clients, which included the United Nations. The UN had commissioned him to create seven short films for its Sustainable Development Summit in New York, one of the largest gatherings of heads of state and world leaders in history.

I asked Sham to help connect me with Jonathan.

"You really don't need me," Sham said. He was sure that once I connected with Jonathan, he'd put together a wonderful film for us. Then he said, "And coincidentally, I'm having lunch with Liesel in London next week."

I was surprised, to say the least. How did Liesel get into this picture? I called Liesel, and she told me that Sham was going to conduct a 360 internal audit for her family office, Blue Haven Initiative.

"What is a 360 audit?" I asked.

"It's when a consultant comes in and examines the organization, top to bottom," she explained. "The consultant interviews everybody who's ever had anything to do with you. They also interview all the employees and recommend how things could be restructured if that's necessary."

"Liesel, I think that is exactly what *we* need for the foundation!" I exclaimed.

I'd been starting to think about the long-term future of the foundation. Eleven years into this project, I was getting more and more concerned that I was, admittedly by design, its sole director. We had no formal board because I never wanted or needed one.

The foundation was incorporated in Delaware as a nonprofit, partly because the rules of incorporation in Delaware required us to have only one director. But the rules are also flexible enough to allow us to change that number at any point.

I had refrained from expanding the board to include anyone other than myself so I could function as nimbly and effectively as possible. That does not mean that others weren't closely involved with my decisions. I never made an important decision without involving my full team and working with them to reach a consensus. But once we agreed on a course of action, like releasing funds, we proceeded quickly since we didn't need to go through a lengthy board approval process.

By 2019, the foundation was very active, and I had started to worry that if something happened to me, our operations would be severely compromised. Having learned what a 360-degree audit entailed, I decided the time was right to employ Sham.

We also hired Jonathan to film our work. Jonathan flew to Ghana and captured footage and conducted many interviews to put together a film that captured the journey of the Rising Schools Program. What resulted was a beautiful and award-winning film that we display on our website.

Sham flew from his home in the UK to Chicago to meet with us and subsequently conducted a multitude of interviews with a great variety of stakeholders. He later returned to share the results of his review with us, which were remarkably insightful and deeply satisfying. The feedback was largely encouraging.

VALIDATED AND INSPIRED: INSIGHTS FROM THE AUDIT

I was truly humbled to learn how effective our efforts to create impactful and trustworthy partnerships had been. Not only had participants confirmed this, but they also encouraged us to create even more partnerships and leverage our success to bring new international partners to the table.

Stakeholders had been asked several questions like, "What if the IDP Foundation disappeared?"

Vincent Amponsah at Sinapi Aba responded, "If IDPF vanishes today, it will slow us down because they are incredible, and they have supported us incredibly. But we will still continue. There is no way we will abandon the Rising Schools Program. No way. The roots are already there."

It was encouraging to learn that our presence was deeply impactful—and that what we had created together would endure regardless.

However, Bernard Ayensu, the principal planning officer for the Ministry of Education in Ghana, told us: "One of the school proprietors in my region asked me, 'If they left now, what would happen?' Of course, I had to give them hope and tell them the ministry would take over and continue. The truth is that is unlikely. If they leave, it would be a loss to me and the ministry, but especially to all these kids who would miss out on a quality education."

We heard similar sentiments from proprietors, such as Joyce Stephenson, proprietor of the Stephenson School, who responded, "Without the IDP Foundation, we would not be able to stay in business. It is that serious. We are low-fee schools; we are not able to buy all the materials that the higher-fee schools can have—but through the training from the IDP Foundation, we are able to make most of these things with our own hands. They are giving us the opportunity to create things on our own. All around, people know the teachers at the Stephenson School are very good because of the IDPF training."

Lily Baah, the proprietor of Baah Memorial School, who had been through the Rising Schools Program and received numerous loans from Sinapi Aba, said, "I will still survive, but it would not be the same. We would not thrive. I believe it isn't money that does everything—but it is the ideas and how you manage them. They give us ideas and training."

Our impact on education in Ghana was undeniable, but I realized that sustaining and expanding our progress required a sharper focus on long-term planning.

In Chicago, when asked what differentiates us from other foundations, Brian Hill from Edovo particularly appreciated our ability to make speedy decisions. "Unquestionably, they are different from other foundations in their ability to move quickly," he said. "It is also a straightforward process, and that is a dream. You can tell with Irene, she doesn't want to stand in our way; she wants to help us succeed, so it's very streamlined. That is so important for early-stage companies. To have the rigor and then move on. Also, to stay close but not harass. She also differs because she is thinking about the world's problems—and asking questions about those and getting feedback. And she is pushing the envelope through her investing."

This was deeply meaningful to me and encouraging. It affirmed my choice to be the foundation's sole director and keep it nimble.

Franklin Cudjoe, the founder and CEO of the Imani Center for Policy and Education, told Sham that we were good partners. Imani is a Ghanaian think tank that releases objective critiques and analyses on a variety of issues, including education. They have become a major influencer in Ghana, and we worked together in our advocacy efforts to shed light on the realities of education in Ghana.

"IDPF is not a common foundation," Franklin told us. "They are very focused. They ensure that whatever decisions they make financially and managerially are sound, and they take into consideration local communities. They are quite respectful of the environment they are working in. They are interested in partnerships, especially with policymakers. They understand that without policy, none of this can come to fruition. Overall, they are not just conscious builders; they are also mindful of the stakeholder communities when it comes to delivering education. They are a respectful organization."

Participants were given ample opportunity to provide suggestions for improvement and criticism of the foundation. We understood that we needed to develop a deeper presence in Ghana by strengthening our in-country team, and we were encouraged to focus on increased development of local advocates for the Rising Schools Program.

Furthermore, we heard that there was a lot of interest in learning what our long-term future plans for the foundation entailed, particularly when it came to leadership. Most importantly, we learned that while the foundation was understood to be complex and wide-ranging in its philanthropic activities, it was the Rising Schools Program that put us on the map and should be considered the centerpiece of our work.

The audit, I felt, was a success, and I was eager to start making changes based on what we had learned. But where to begin?

CHARTING THE NEXT CHAPTER

I got on the phone with one of our consultants, Peter Colenso, who was in the UK. He used to work for the Children's International Investment Fund (CIIF), an offshoot of DFID (the British version of USAID—the United States Agency for International Development).

I knew Peter well from education work at CIFF and networking events. When CIFF shifted away from education, my team and I were shocked to learn his departure was imminent. I immediately emailed him, inviting him to join us.

Allison Lawshe walked across the room, laughing, and she said, "I saw his email, and I thought it would take about thirty seconds before you asked him to come and work for us."

Peter responded quickly to my email. "That's really generous," he said. "And I'm very flattered. But truthfully, I would rather look for a position in a large organization like the World Bank than at a smaller foundation like yours."

And I said, "Well, in the meantime, how would you like to do a bit of consulting?" And he said, "Yes, I would love that."

I wasted no time asking for Peter's perspective on the 360 review, in which he had also participated. Over the course of a single phone call, he offered enough suggestions to lead to a complete reorganization of the foundation's operations.

"Irene, do you know, with reading the whole 360-review package and everything, I think you should run this entire program—the Rising Schools Program, that is—out of Ghana," Peter told me. "You already have an in-country director there, Stephen. He's excellent. Promote him to country director for the Rising Schools Program and make it his show. And then he will be able to hire and create the staff and set up offices," he suggested. "You really need international recognition, alliances, and advocacy," Peter said. "And I think that should be the focus of the Chicago office."

I consulted with Allison Lawshe and Alison Ehlke in Chicago and spoke with Liesel. Everyone agreed that Peter's advice was excellent. My next step was to call Stephen Opuni and ask him whether he was interested in the proposition. He wasn't just interested; he was thrilled.

"We do actually have to set up a whole IDP Foundation infrastructure in Ghana," I told him—and he set to work at once. Alison Ehlke would sort out the legal work and the payroll setup from Chicago. She also had to make sure that we understood all the Ghanaian human resources issues. The labor laws in Ghana are, not unsurprisingly, very different from those in the United States. In the meantime, in Ghana, Stephen began to interview administrative assistants and set up our first formal office in Accra.

Peter's suggestion turned out to be brilliant. The decision to conduct a 360-degree audit was catalytic. It was now time to get back to thinking about longevity and building international partnerships, and we began to have discussions about this in Chicago.

One morning in late 2019, Allison Lawshe walked into my office and told me that it might be a good time for her to transition out. She said, "I am not sure I'm the person who is best suited to create international recognition and develop the alliances and advocacy platforms that Peter Colenso envisions."

Allison had been with us for nine and a half years, so it was a deeply emotional moment. She had been an important member of our team and had been wonderfully effective in supporting me as I built the program. She offered to stay with us while we searched for her replacement and offered to work in a consulting capacity to facilitate a smooth handoff to whoever was chosen to be our new executive director of education. She had an enormous amount of institutional experience to pass on to her replacement. I was, and remain, deeply grateful to her for her passion, her engagement, and how professionally and supportively she managed her departure from the foundation.

We hired an excellent global search firm to look for her replacement. I thought it would be highly advantageous for the new director to be based in England since it is conveniently accessible to both Ghana, the East Coast of the United States, and Chicago. Also, if we really wanted to engage a global constituency to help pressure governments to be more inclusive of low-fee private schools, many of the foundations and organizations we needed assistance from were based in Europe.

The search was underway. I was truly excited by the new direction we were taking. My whole approach to the foundation had been reenergized and reinvigorated. The Rising Schools Program, meanwhile, had reached a remarkable eight-hundred-plus schools and now had an astonishing loan repayment rate of 97 percent.

As 2019 drew to a close, I felt that our momentum was unstoppable.

And then the whole world turned upside down.

In January 2020, rumors started to leak out from China that there was a flu-like virus spreading rapidly. It was thought to have originated in a Wuhan wet market. Rumor soon gave way to fact as the virus worked its way ferociously around the world. By early March 2020, most of the world had gone into lockdown in hopes of slowing the spread of COVID-19 until effective measures could be taken to protect the global population.

As I sat in my apartment, I obsessed about Ghana. *What was going to happen to our schools?*

Initially, the Ghanaian staff believed that the pandemic would not affect Africa, that it would confine itself to the West. Stephen told me that they were all unprepared for the lockdown. However, on March 15, 2020, the government of Ghana instituted a partial lockdown, banning all public gatherings. All schools and universities were shut down.

"All of a sudden, one Sunday evening the president shows up in a public announcement and says schools are closing," Stephen told us. "There was no warning for proprietors or school leaders to even think about putting structures in place to protect their school classrooms—including perishable supplies that were in the schools—or to think of a way of managing them. So that Sunday evening, schools were closed. We were not prepared for this kind of global pandemic, and we had not prepared the proprietors for closures. Our partners had no chance to prepare for what was to come."

Chapter 10

SUCCESS AND SUCCESSION

With the world at a complete standstill and our program hanging in limbo, we nevertheless started the interview process to replace Allison Lawshe, the program manager for the Rising Schools Program. Her replacement would hold the title of director of education and work closely with the Ghanaian team. This person would also be tasked with building new partnerships and making new alliances, in line with Peter Colenso's strategic guidance.

Because of the lockdown, all interviews had to be conducted via Zoom, a new experience for me. The primary search committee consisted of seven people, including our consultants, the search firm, key staff members, and me.

I was in awe of the quality of the candidates our search firm was bringing to the table, and it made me think. One of the key takeaways from the 360-degree review was that we needed to think seriously about the future, and to me, that also encompassed the question of succession. I went to the recruiters and raised the idea

> No prosperous nation is an uneducated nation.

that not only would our new hire be director of education, but that same person might eventually become CEO of the IDP Foundation.

As a cofounder responsible for leading the IDP Foundation from its inception, I'd become aware that most people in my position have a problem letting go. It was interesting to see how surprised everybody was when I announced that I was ready to begin implementing a succession plan.

One of the marks of a good leader is recognizing when it's time for your role to evolve, when you realize that what you created needs someone with a whole different skill set to carry the work forward. This is essential if you want the work you have accomplished to continue, succeed, and have impact.

In fact, particularly with family foundations, there is a well-known phenomenon called "founder's syndrome," which prevents leaders from stepping away from the organization or foundation they created even when it is clear that the organization needs fresh ideas. It's why a lot of organizations stagnate or fail.

PLANNING FOR GROWTH AND EVOLUTION:
STRENGTHENING THE TEAM FOR FUTURE SUCCESS

We knew that it was important to spread the word internationally about what we had accomplished and were continuing to do. I wanted to impress upon governments in the developing world the importance of low-fee private schools to the overall educational health of their nations. No prosperous nation is an uneducated nation.

Our work and platform certainly got attention. But how does one effectively advertise this? After fifteen years of tremendously challenging work in Ghana, I thought that if we were to expand into other countries, I had better ensure that a very energetic person joined our team in a very senior capacity!

The COVID-19 crisis served as a stark reminder of life's fragility. It prompted me to contemplate the potential ramifications for the IDP Foundation and our mission in the event of unforeseen circumstances affecting me. The repercussions for the Rising Schools Program in Ghana alone were daunting, not to mention the challenges of expanding the model to other countries. Without a comprehensive plan in place, everything could come to a halt. Recognizing the need to relinquish some control, I was prepared to acknowledge this reality. Amid the grimness of the pandemic, one silver lining emerged— the operational pause and the ongoing hiring process presented a unique opportunity to implement significant and necessary changes.

As a part of the succession process, I wrote a document that I called "The Founder's Intent." It represented my wish for the future of the foundation and how to adapt to a rapidly changing world. It was important to consider the possibility that the Rising Schools Programs might one day be unnecessary. Somewhere down the road it might no longer be the most relevant thing on which to concentrate. What if the government of Ghana were to find itself in a position to expand public schools to the point where low-fee private schools were no longer necessary? Or if it began to substantially increase support for these schools? Were that to happen, then the foundation had to be free to change courses and find new areas of focus and new ways to operate. I wanted our new leadership to have the ability to take the foundation in a sensible direction and not be wedded to any single idea.

Meanwhile, the pandemic raged on. We all hoped that it would all be over in two months, but two months stretched into May. It was becoming clearer and clearer that the pandemic was going to take a long time to clear. *Perhaps it will be over by the fall?*

Death rates were increasing—and alarming. We prayed for the rapid creation of a vaccine. We would not be able to create "a new normal" until increased immunity diminished the most severe effects of the virus. However, during all this, our hiring process continued.

A frontrunner began to emerge. Corina Gardner had a bachelor of arts in political science from the University of California, Berkeley, and a master of business administration from the University of Cambridge. Her previous work experience included four years working with GSMA, a company dedicated to "unifying the mobile ecosystem to discover, develop, and deliver innovation foundational to positive business environments and societal change." She had also been the director for global strategy at the Nike Foundation's Girl Effect, among other positions.

When initially contacted by the search firm, she had no interest in applying, since she assumed that working for a foundation would involve significant fundraising. She also wanted to avoid being caught in a never-ending series of unrealistic expectations from a board and staff accustomed to the foundation working in a certain way. The recruiter got on the phone and explained to Corina that she needn't worry about these downsides—they didn't exist at the IDP Foundation.

Corina asked about the focus on market dynamics. "Yes," she was told, "it's a nonprofit, but the foundation works within the market. In fact, the specific model that Irene has developed is incredibly market-driven and dynamic." After these initial discussions, Corina became more interested in the position.

In many ways, she was an outsider candidate. She had little experience in education, but once her passion, intellectual ferocity, and drive became apparent, I had few reservations about hiring her. And I knew it wouldn't take long for her to familiarize herself with how our programs functioned.

In June 2020, we hired Corina as our new director of education. I wanted her to get to Ghana as soon as possible—because I knew that would be an education in itself—and she was also itching to go and see what it was like on the ground. Of course, with a lockdown in place, she was confined to her home. However, because the program was essentially frozen, our staff had the time to engage with her via Zoom and bring her up to speed with our operations. She voraciously read every note, report, and file ever created for the IDP Foundation. I was deeply impressed.

We hoped that the pandemic would ease enough so that we might see a reopening of schools by September. But September passed and drifted into October, and then November—and still no reopening. By this point I wondered how we would ever recover. If there were no schools open, proprietors couldn't collect fees to cover their ongoing expenses and their outstanding loans to Sinapi Aba. It was a complete and utter mess.

December 2020 saw the first glimmer of hope. The Ghanaian government let students who were testing at the junior high level come back to complete their exams. And in January 2021, nine months after the outbreak of the pandemic, Ghanaian schools were allowed to reopen with numerous protective measures and protocols to ensure student safety.

Over the course of the lockdown, reports were shared with us as to how our proprietors were faring under such impossible circumstances. Lily Baah, the proprietor of Baah Memorial School outside of Kumasi and one of the stars of our program, had started a business selling homemade bread and made-to-order pies.

"I started with the pie and the biscuits and bread," she told us. "But I would finish baking the pie, and it was so hard you could crack it with a hammer only. So, I turned things around by making children's clothes. And that helped a lot. I even had one lady coming from Sunyani to buy from me and another one from, I think, Cape Coast, Central Region, and I sold some myself in the markets."

She also sewed bedsheets crafted from local fabrics. She used the proceeds to pay the salaries of her teachers, who in the meantime were using WhatsApp to stay in touch with their students. Prior to the lockdown, Lily had increased her enrollment to 584 students, but even in the former robust economic climate, she had found it difficult to meet her financial requirements. The lockdown pushed her to the brink of collapse—and other proprietors, who weren't as resourceful as Lily, were in even worse shape.

We had to start working out ways to help some of the more vulnerable schools in our program. We believed that helping them dig themselves out of a situation that was completely out of their control was a moral obligation for the foundation.

Globally, it has been estimated that 258 million children of primary- and secondary-school age were not enrolled in school before the pandemic.[*] That number was poised to increase dramatically if the low-fee private schools responsible for educating an increasing number of the world's poorest children were unable to

---

[*] UNESCO Institute for Statistics, "Out-of-School Children and Youth," accessed April 14, 2025, https://uis.unesco.org/en/topic/out-school-children-and-youth.

reopen. After over a decade of helping support such schools in Ghana, our work would come to nothing if we were to lose them to the economic ravages of the pandemic.

We commissioned Associates for Change (AFC), an Accra-based research and consulting firm, to assess the impact of the pandemic on our schools. They reported that approximately 15 percent of low-fee private schools faced imminent bankruptcy and an additional 65 percent were at risk of closing unless they received urgent financial aid. None of these schools received any COVID-related support from the government or international aid agencies.

We were hearing increasingly from proprietors who were part of the Rising Schools Program that they expected dire consequences from the shutdown. We heard from Magdalene Sackey, one such proprietor, who shared, "Government teachers were being paid, but the private schools were left out. If I am home and I'm not running my school, where do I get extra funds to pay my teachers? I think the government should help. Even if it wasn't something huge, just something meager would help."

"When the lockdown began, whatever funds I had I used to pay the teachers," Lily Baah told us. "I was able to sustain this for five months until I ran out of money. Then I started my outside business. But it wasn't enough to sustain us."

Could she survive? She had tried to use available technology to maintain contact with her students. "We quickly put together our virtual classrooms," she said. "We sent our students exercises and lectures through the phones. Where we had a problem was most of the parents didn't have phones. So, when we sent the work, they might end up getting it two or three days later because they had to go and get somebody else's phone or computer to retrieve the work."

Her story was not unique. Distance learning was out of the question for most families. Parents either didn't own equipment (phones, computers, etc.), or if they did, they couldn't afford the data plans to keep their children virtually "in school" all day.

"We also tried online programs," Magdalene Sackey told us, "but the kids here are not so used to online teaching. So, it was a challenge. And the parents themselves were not able to help. 'Madam, I barely have money to buy data to come online at all,' they would tell us. And the children who were able to join us online were used to one-on-one time in a classroom, so this format wasn't effective for them. We would sign on, but then we would have just one or two children joining."

The Ministry of Education and Ghana Education Service (GES) had introduced remote learning programs, but not all were successful. AFC reported that only 5 percent of students accessed Ghana's online learning channel during the shutdowns, while 11 percent and 18 percent accessed state-sponsored radio and TV learning channels, respectively.

Despite the lack of online engagement, there was clearly a strong desire to keep the educational process moving. We were hearing many stories of teachers going around and physically checking in on learners, even though this was in violation of Ghana's very strict COVID restrictions. Alternatively, some parents were lucky enough to have teachers in the family offer homeschooling.

The lockdown was tight in Ghana. There were active enforcers roaming the streets with guns to make sure that people were not out and about. People who were intent on keeping some learning going and educating their kids took considerable risk if they ignored restrictions.

IDPF Country Director Stephen Opuni shared with me one story of an enterprising proprietor. "To make sure that she didn't lose children and parents," he said, "she took it upon herself to visit a couple of children every single day. She left her house, masked up, and went around to all the homes that her students are coming from, and then she shared a little bit of information with the parents on how to keep their children learning and engaged." Stephen later told me that when schools reopened, her efforts paid off: A good number of her students and teachers returned to school, which was not the case for many of our other schools.

NAVIGATING THE CRISIS:
ENSURING SCHOOLS' SURVIVAL AND RECOVERY

Throughout the lockdown, we kept in constant contact with Sinapi Aba to come up with solutions to ensure that our schools wouldn't crack underneath the burdens created by the lack of income and the responsibility of their debt. Who could ever have planned for the fallout from COVID? We had to step in to prevent the program, which we had worked so hard to create, from failing. Even though we did not expect to make more grants, priding ourselves on the degree of sustainability that we had achieved, we needed to make some rapid decisions to prevent the whole program from imploding. Luckily, because of the way the foundation is structured, we were able to implement creative ways to save the program.

First, we agreed to put the loans on hold. Wherever proprietors were in their loan cycles, the repayments would stop and pick back up when schools reopened. We communicated that immediately to all proprietors. We also needed interest to stop accruing during the moratorium on payments. So, we negotiated an agreement with

Sinapi Aba. When schools reopened, the IDP Foundation would give a grant to Sinapi Aba to cover all the interest that schools had accrued during the closures. This was certainly not the business model we had created—we thought that we would not need to provide any more grants for the Rising Schools Program—but the crisis we were experiencing was unprecedented.

Under the terms of the agreement, whatever the proprietor's debt profile was at the time of the shutdown, it would be the same when they reopened, so they wouldn't be any worse off. All this news was gratefully received by both proprietors and Sinapi Aba.

We also knew that schools would be in various states of readiness when it came time to reopen. Even though they weren't accruing any interest on their loans, they were still facing the consequences of being without income for ten months. Many lost staff and teachers who had been forced to find other jobs to survive. In addition, most schools would likely see a decline in enrollment.

There were additional formal government requirements for the schools to reopen safely. There were new protocols, including providing masks and hand sanitizer and following social-distancing guidelines. This would create problems for the schools that had limited space or whose furniture and infrastructure were basic at best.

Among GES's new safety requirements was limiting the number of students who could sit at the same desk. So not having enough desks suddenly became a major concern. Also, it wasn't unusual for kids to be seated on the floor at schools where infrastructure improvements were still being made. But the government mandated that students would no longer be permitted to sit on an earthen floor post-COVID.

Sinapi Aba really shone. They had cultivated a true partnership and close relationship with the schools they served; their loan officers, as I've noted, had developed direct, tight relationships with school proprietors through their training. They knew the schools well. They had visited them and stayed in touch with them.

Along with our AFC study, we asked Sinapi Aba to conduct a quick audit of the situation in collaboration with Raphael Akomeah. We wanted to learn about the circumstances that the schools found themselves in. The auditors developed a sort of scorecard so that we could understand what level of need our schools were facing. We asked, "What are the basic requirements that would be needed in order to reopen and meet all of the infrastructure and hygiene requirements?"

The scorecards showed us that we had to act—and act quickly—if we were to support the most vulnerable schools in our program.

One of the hardest things to do in development is to give small amounts of money to people or to respond to very specific needs at moments of crisis. Sometimes the smaller the grant is, the harder it is to disburse because no matter how little money you give, there is still a certain amount of due diligence, oversight, management, and paperwork that's required.

In most cases, foundations and donors end up going through a cost-versus-impact negotiation. If more time is spent on a loan and more paperwork is generated, then more money should be going out of the door—and there's the opinion that large grants that take more time to prepare should go to a larger constituency. On the other hand, a single proprietor's need for a five-hundred-dollar grant to buy the number of desks they need to open their school safely is the kind of request that can easily slip through the cracks and get lost without receiving the consideration it deserves. Institutions are accustomed to doling out large grants—and here our proprietors couldn't borrow even five hundred dollars because they already owed money to Sinapi Aba.

However, I wasn't going to balk at the cost in time and effort of paperwork for small grants to individuals. "Just do it," I said. "We're not going to have our hands tied by our own red tape, ever."

I discussed the situation at length with Corina. To mitigate the financial strain facing the schools, we stepped in for a second time. I ordered the foundation to launch an immediate relief effort to be facilitated by Sinapi Aba. In the end, 144 schools (serving 41,000 students) received support. A good number of schools were awarded need-based grants of around US$2,488 per school. Including the grant to Sinapi Aba to cover the lapsed loan interest, the final tally of the total funds allocated was a little more than US$365,000. The funding impacted over nine hundred teachers. Sixty-six percent of grant recipients cited support of teacher salaries as a primary need.

Other needs also had to be addressed. For ten months, most of the schools had been sitting empty, and some had fallen into disrepair. This was true for school-owned vehicles as well. And classroom furniture, teaching and learning supplies, personal protective equipment, and canteen items were also high priorities. Additionally, many of the schools had been looted during the lockdown.

As schools started to reopen, Associates for Change noted that 50 percent of the low-fee private schools had initial low enrollment because many students transferred to a public school, entered the workforce, or, in some cases, were pregnant or had given birth.

Ultimately, we were amazed by the resilience of our schools. Whereas we expected to see a high number of school closures, in the end, only two schools of the seven hundred that we checked on had permanently closed—and it is likely that these two troubled schools would have closed with or without a pandemic. For them, COVID just accelerated the inevitable.

Most of the clients who make up our portfolio are perceived as high-risk clients who other banks or creditors would hesitate to support. By their standards, we should have seen a high fail rate. But though there's a common *perception* of our schools being at high risk, they rarely fail, even under extreme circumstances. If there's a problem that we do have, it's one of perceptions, not an *actual* problem: Over 98 percent of our proprietors repay their loans, a rate that has been consistent since the inception of the program after we completed the pilot.

I am certain that our training programs contributed to the resiliency of our schools. There is no more important time for strong financial management and accounting—making a little go a long way—than in a crisis. Thanks to their financial training, many of our proprietors had accumulated enough cash reserves to see themselves through at least a part of the lockdown. After reopening, when we interviewed the school proprietors who were recipients of our grants, they all pointed toward accumulating savings as their highest priority moving forward.

That said, for the schools that needed grants, our engagement was a lifesaver. Imranah Adams, monitoring, evaluation, and learning manager at the IDP Foundation, reported, "If we hadn't come in as an organization, a number of these schools would have collapsed. During monitoring visits after reopening, you could see in the faces of the proprietors and even the schoolchildren a sense of joy. A lot of them told me that they hadn't experienced such a gesture before in their lives. They had never envisioned IDPF coming in to rescue them."

LEADERSHIP AND TRANSFORMATION POST-PANDEMIC

On one of our team calls, Constance Kwaa Ababio, policy and advocacy manager for the IDP Foundation, observed an unexpected benefit in the aftermath of the pandemic. "I feel that now proprietors have become more aware that they need to be visible," she said. "They need to be together; they need to engage. It's not enough to just sit in the corner, continue to do things on your own, and expect that things will improve."

She explained how the pandemic shifted their perspective. "When COVID arrived, they really began to value the essence of togetherness. When the government launched COVID relief support, proprietors had to be aligned with a private school association to get information on how to even apply for relief funding.

"This helped them realize that they could not do this alone," she continued, "and that they needed to actively engage and be more involved with the private school association. Prior to COVID, because of regulatory issues and standards, most of them didn't want to be exposed, so they hid in their own corner, doing their own thing," she said.

"And now," she added with a note of optimism, "I see the enthusiasm and the willingness of most of these schools to actually register with the government."

"It was a reality check for everybody," added Stephen Opuni, who was our country director at the time and later became our regional director, "because after ten months of school closures where you're not getting support from anywhere other than such limited programs as ours, you then ask yourself the difficult question, *Is it worth continuing this?* And if you don't have passion, I think you would stop. But there's currently a revamped passion to grow. We've experienced a lot of new loan requests and interest in our program. And people are really rebuilding. As a funder, we are very passionate about supporting our partners in this journey to really build back better and support them in realizing some of the bigger questions around learning. I think this is an exciting new horizon for us."

Meanwhile, Corina was finally able to make her first trip to Ghana in June 2021. I flew to London to accompany her on the flight so I would be able to share as much as possible of what I had learned in my years in the field—and person-to-person. In the over three weeks she spent in Ghana, she traveled around and became familiar with the full scope of our operations and the ways in which I had engaged with our team to date.

At her six-month review, I felt that I had passed on enough knowledge about the functions of the foundation so that I felt comfortable expanding her role. I gave Corina the title of executive director, a title connoting more authority. I wanted to empower her to make the kind of connections she had been hired to create. Titles are important, particularly for women who are often marginalized despite their obvious competence.

I was extremely anxious that the innovative product that we had created with Sinapi Aba, which we had proven was a sustainable model, would be recognized and expanded to a global platform. For that, we needed a CEO, and Corina seemed the obvious choice. The position would give Corina the force she needed to build important new partnerships and promote the foundation as a leader in the field, two goals that went hand in hand and would enable us to shine an even brighter light on the enormous contributions low-fee private schools were making to the education sector.

I decided to offer Corina the role of CEO and make myself chair of the board. Once again, I was grateful that I could make decisions like these without the burden of navigating the process with an unwieldy board. Working with a large board might have taken months and involved innumerable committees and board meetings. During our earlier, very thorough international search to bring Corina on board, in which a large share of my team participated, due diligence had already been conducted.

Once that was done, I decided to finally create a small board. Liesel agreed to accept formal membership on the board, and eventually Corina was also appointed as a voting member. Adding myself, that brought the total board membership to three—still small, but well informed and still very nimble.

Meantime, there was much to be done in establishing a London base, sustaining the Ghana office, and, of course, keeping our Chicago office up-to-date on all developments. Alison Ehlke, our chief operating officer, had to navigate the enormous task of sorting out a multitude of organizational structures in three vastly different countries.

As we wrestled with the new format, given the CEO's comprehensive mandate to take our model to gain global recognition and form collaborative partnerships with other funders, it made sense to also assign the educational budget to Corina. My daughter and I, recalling our initial impulse as cofounders, decided that I should have my own budget to continue to support medical research and other community initiatives from my base in Chicago.

As I look forward to seeing what we do next—what new directions the team leads us in—all I can say is that it has been a remarkable journey thus far, a journey that began with my impassioned and indignant response to the lack of equal educational opportunities I observed in Ghana on those early visits. I am proud of all that the IDP Foundation has accomplished since then.

I am also proud that I realized that the scope of the job was too big for me before it was too late. Hanging on and clinging to power for too long can cause a foundation to fail in its objectives, leaving an overwhelming mess in its wake. I saw that, and I knew that I didn't want to be responsible for the failure of something I loved.

In mid-2022, we received the best possible news from Sinapi Aba. They informed us that they would be able to continue running the Rising Schools Program without further funding from the IDP Foundation. They had disbursed all the recent IDPF funding and were now using their own funds to disburse loans to both new and existing schools. Despite one of the worst economic shocks in the history of the world—Ghana was particularly hard hit by the pandemic—they are continuing to expand the program. New schools are taking out new loans. Sinapi Aba is very committed, and market demand only grows.

We have created a proven business model and a program that has moved away from aid. Against all odds, we now have a sustainable program.

Chapter 11

CREATING A GLOBAL PRESENCE

With our business model a proven success in 2024, it was time to start exploring other markets. In Ghana, we had helped more than one thousand schools to improve their infrastructure by providing training and giving some proprietors access to business loans that they would not, by any stretch of the imagination, have been able to secure otherwise. We had a repayment rate just short of 100 percent. Most importantly, for most, if not all, of these schools, the engagement of the Rising Schools Program had been nothing less than transformative. The training received from Sinapi Aba had an indelible impact on the way they operated, producing in turn life-changing improvements for the children attending those schools. The Rising Schools Program has already given thousands of children hope for the future, and now we have a powerful opportunity to expand our recognition and impact—reaching hundreds of thousands more by rolling out this model to additional countries.

> One of the keys to the success of our program was that we learned from local input rather than sweeping in with our Western ideas of how things should be done.

In addition, the advocacy work we carried out over the sixteen years since the launch of the Rising Schools Program has led to significant shifts in both perception and practice. Other education stakeholders have been watching our progress with great interest, and many of them are now coming to the IDP Foundation for advice. These organizations can see the market potential of our approach and see value in our years of experience, research, and data. Our success cannot be denied. The repayment rates and the wide-scale adoption of our methodology speak for themselves.

In retrospect, we were decidedly ahead of our time, especially in our philosophy of working from local knowledge and information. One of the keys to the success of our program was that we learned from local input rather than sweeping in with our Western ideas of how things should be done.

This work has now led us to collaborate with major international development organizations in creating a significant new Generation Empowerment Fund. Its purpose is to empower a whole new generation of proprietors and students through focused interventions, which will include providing financing to replicate our model across sub-Saharan Africa.

Population growth in Africa in the last twelve years has been exponential, outstripping the ability of governments to build and fund schools for millions of children. Today, low-fee private schools represent around 30 percent of schools on the continent. The reality is that a lack of access to quality education has created an organic, community-driven response. There is movement away from long-held debates around public versus private schools. The sheer quantity of low-fee private schools proves that they are a critical component in realizing the world's education goals, and we have no time to wait for public education systems to catch up to the increasing demand for quality education.

ONGOZA: LEADING THE WAY IN KENYA

Building on the success of the Rising Schools Program in Ghana, we were thrilled to take the next step in our journey, bringing the program to Kenya and opening the door to new opportunities and growth. However, starting the program in Kenya was a considerably different experience than our work in Ghana. As previously mentioned, the proliferation of low-fee private schools is considerable, and the schools themselves are recognizable as being viable customers for business loans. We no longer had to incentivize financial institutions to make loans to low-fee private schools by providing them with grant funding. We now have a proven model, and the word was out about the financial success. Institutions were now approaching us and asking for technical support. This meant we could start a new partnership with a much stronger financial position. In Kenya, we provided a low-interest loan worth US$1 million and required that it be matched with another US$2 million of commercial capital, setting standards of what kinds of schools they could on-lend the full US$3 million. This ensured that we would still be able to reach schools that were most in need but still considered to be high-risk prospects.

Being led by our local partners has always been at the heart of everything we do, so we asked our Kenyan partners to create a name for the program that would resonate with school leaders and parents. They chose "Ongoza," which means "lead" in Kiswahili, and it was under this name that we launched the IDPF Ongoza Program in Kenya in 2022.

The financial institution we partnered with for this program in Kenya, Premier Credit, offers loan products almost identical to those we developed with Sinapi Aba in Ghana. As with the Rising Schools Program, school owners are given access to Premier Credit's low-interest school improvement loans, alongside training on effective management of school finances and record keeping.

There are estimated to be over seven thousand nonformal Alternative Providers of Basic Education and Training (APBET) schools across Kenya. These low-fee private schools are responsible for educating over two million learners. Like Ghana, most of the children attending these schools are from extremely marginalized backgrounds. Also, while 90 percent of teachers at public schools in Kenya are certified by the Teachers Service Commission (TSC), 90 percent of their counterparts working in low-fee private schools are not (as of 2024).

A key benefit of launching the IDPF Ongoza Program after so many years of monitoring, evaluating, and learning with the Rising Schools Program in Ghana was that we weren't starting from scratch. The challenges faced and lessons learned in Ghana played a key role in the setup of our second country program. With over a decade of experience under our belts, we were able to reach more schools at a much faster pace. By applying our earned knowledge and insights from Ghana, by year two the program had reached five hundred schools and administered over one thousand individual loans, surpassing our total reach over the sixteen years in

Ghana. The speed at which the program was implemented in the low-fee private school market in Kenya illustrates the enormous market demand.

Following the completion of the training program, more schools began using digital payments or M-Pesa for school-fee collection. As we had learned in Ghana, collecting school fees can be a significant challenge for proprietors. However, the training and subsequent switch from collecting cash to online services allowed schools to considerably increase their rates of collection.

Furthermore, the training helped schools diversify their revenue streams, resulting in a 59 percent increase in schools establishing additional sources of income such as selling school uniforms, hiring out the school bus, renting out their premises, and running extracurricular activities, from school trips to swimming classes.

Just as with our work in Ghana, proprietors learned to separate school finances from their personal finances. This resulted in a 40 percent increase in school owners finding the means to pay themselves a set salary, along with the ability to keep up with teacher salaries. An impressive 43 percent of schools began using cash-flow plans.

As the IDPF Ongoza Program continued to grow, we carried forward lessons from our work in Ghana. In early 2024, we brought a team from Premier Credit to Ghana to tour Rising Schools Program sites alongside a team from Sinapi Aba. While we knew that the Premier Credit team understood in detail our accomplishments with the Rising Schools Program, seeing the program succeed in action clearly left a lasting impression on them. They shared that one of their most important takeaways came from observing loan officers really engaging with proprietors and giving financial literacy training. The proprietors saw their loan officers not as debt collectors but as friendly and supportive business partners. The Premier Credit team realized that they too could create these kinds of relationships in their own schools in Kenya.

The personal approach created a completely different sense of self-worth, value, and motivation for the loan officers. The team was clearly hungry to re-create the model at Premier Credit, and they got to work immediately.

We sent the Sinapi Aba team to Kenya, where they directly trained our financial partners in how to gain trust and better support proprietors. This international collaboration had the happy result of aligning the two programs much more closely.

NATIONAL ADVOCACY IN GHANA

Strengthening the Role of Low-Fee Private Schools in Policy

Sinapi Aba continues to roll out loans in Ghana and is still entirely self-sustaining. While the Rising Schools Program continues to evolve in Ghana, our focus has expanded to include national advocacy efforts, ensuring broader support and recognition for the private school sector.

We always focus on supporting local ingenuity from the entrepreneurial spirit of school owners to lead in the areas of policy and government accountability. This dual approach of supporting schools and identifying local engineers of systems change is integral to our work. While the Rising Schools Program has changed the low-fee private school landscape, enabling more schools to reach more children, we also support the advocacy work of the Ghanaian National

Association of Private Schools (GNAPS). The organization was formed in 1973 as a nonpolitical and nonsectarian body.

While there are close to fifty organizations that provide services and advocacy for a collection of private schools, GNAPS represents the largest body of private school owners at the pre-tertiary level in Ghana. It advocates for the recognition of these schools in Ghana, promoting and protecting their economic and social interests and supporting their development and management. It also serves as an information link between Ghana Education Service (GES) and public and private schools within Ghana's many districts.

When I first arrived in Ghana to begin the work of the foundation, GNAPS was in urgent need of recognition and support. As the work of the Rising Schools Program grew, we began to see how important GNAPS could be to the health of the schools we were supporting, particularly given my belief in the necessity for collaboration with the government. Therefore, IDPF provided GNAPS with funding to strengthen its internal structures and staffing to allow for greater advocacy. This capacity-building helped GNAPS revise its constitution, develop a strategic plan, engage critical staff at the national secretariat, champion media campaigns, and undertake further-reaching advocacy. As a result of this partnership, GNAPS now sits in an advisory role on the government's technical working group, informing policy related to licensing and management of private schools.

With this seat at the table, they work with the government to increase registration rates and improve the visibility of private schools by addressing barriers that have kept schools from formally registering with the government. As a result, the paperwork and registration processes have been simplified, the fees for initial registration have been lowered, and at the time of writing, a new sliding scale of registration fees is under consideration to reflect the income level of the communities in which the schools serve. We continue to see the impact of their successful advocacy with an impressive list of accomplishments which include the removal of the NaSIA's (National Schools Inspectorate Authority) annual school license renewal fees. GNAPS also managed to bring about the inclusion of private schools in the National Standardized Test, an initiative to assess the learning outcomes of Primary 2 and Primary 4 pupils initially designed exclusively for public schools. This move toward greater inclusion of all schools in the bearing of government was a significant milestone.

Empowering Teachers, Elevating Standards

While creating greater access to education for all children is at the heart of our work, this has always been underpinned by a desire to achieve better learning outcomes. In 2024, we set out to improve standards of education with a new initiative.

The Techniques for Effective Teaching (TFET) program that we created with the Sesame Workshop has been very well received by proprietors and teachers. You might remember that TFET had been adopted into the Ghanaian teacher training process. TFET was years ahead of its time. It introduces numerous proactive rather than retributive approaches to classroom management. However, learning outcomes were still not significantly improving. While it is crucial to help learners find their confidence and provide them with strong engagement tools, if they can't sufficiently read when they leave school, those techniques are rendered useless. The number of learners leaving primary school who were unable to read was unacceptably high. It was essential to introduce new techniques into the Rising Schools Program to address this perpetuating learning crisis.

Following the core values of IDPF to empower those who are on the ground tackling education issues, we began to search for implementers who were focused on improving learning outcomes rather than trying to create an intervention from scratch.

We partnered with a group of tenured professors who delivered TFET in teacher training colleges across Ghana, and we learned that many of them were supplementing their income with side jobs. This gave us an idea! We suggested that if they were to create their own company, we could work with them to help train teachers in our schools. With our encouragement, they did just that, creating a limited company called the Centre for Professional Development, Training, and Education (CPDTE).

CPDTE then paired up with Inspiring Teachers, another organization dedicated to helping teachers improve learning in low-resource contexts. Together they designed an updated program that included all the original techniques covered in TFET but with an entirely new approach to delivery and support. The content and materials were all newly created to reflect the current curriculum and best practices. In April 2024, we formally announced the new initiative, calling it Tools for Foundational Learning Improvement (TFLI), which was piloted and then launched across many schools with plans to increase its placement in the following years.

I am highly impressed with TFLI's potential to scale at the national level. Over many years, I have been exposed to a multitude of teaching and learning interventions that I never felt had the potential to scale in a meaningful way, but TFLI is different. Through robust materials and government buy-in and support, TFLI can scale with great impact.

In 2022, the government of Ghana passed a law making it illegal for schools to use untrained teachers. While the deadline for registration and licensure was set at the end of 2024, low-fee private schools immediately became vulnerable to being shut down if they continued employing untrained teachers. However, a massive teacher shortage exists in Ghana. Today nearly a third of all children are being, at least partially, taught by untrained teachers. Equally, the formal route to becoming a teacher is a pathway that is not open to most. With less than 10 percent of the population enrolling in tertiary education, a very small and elite pool of Ghanaians can service the country's trained teacher needs.

We immediately perceived this as an opportunity to support low-fee private school teachers while aligning with the government's drive to get untrained teachers qualified and licensed. The two main barriers are cost and time. Most simply cannot take the time away from their teaching to embark upon a two-year full-time training process. We surmised that should TFLI be recognized by the government as delivering many of the same skills being taught in teacher training courses, we could get low-fee private school teachers' credit toward their formal qualification.

This initiative was launched with an IDPF grant, and additional funding from other foundations has since supported its growth. We committed to a four-year funding cycle, and we know how important it is that the initiative receives government recognition.

We are also in the early stages of designing a new loan product to pay for the training. We are theorizing that loan repayment could be shared by the school and the teachers. This means TFLI would no longer be dependent on philanthropic or donor funding to scale. Schools will benefit from improved teaching quality in real time as teachers undergo TFLI training. With recognition from the National Teaching Council, early career teachers may also earn points toward full certification.

The loan, which covers the cost of the TFLI training, would be repaid over several years by both the school proprietor and through deductions from the teacher's salary. This arrangement is designed to help solve another common problem school proprietors face—high teacher attrition. Today, there is often a disincentive for proprietors to invest in training their teachers, as the assumption is that once the training is complete, the teacher will go to a higher-paying school. However, if the certification attached to the training is conditional and based on repayment of the loan, then the teacher will stay for at least the repayment period, and their relationship with the school proprietor will solidify because of their subsidizing the cost of the certification. So, a win-win situation!

GRASSROOTS ADVOCACY

As I have repeatedly stated, I believe government involvement and cooperation are essential to the success of any education venture. So, in cooperation with the Global Schools Forum, we created the All Hands On Deck toolkit. The toolkit serves as a template that can be accessed by educators all around the world to create effective partnerships and collaborations in education systems. It is easily adaptable to suit any context.

To create the toolkit, we engaged the services of Oxford Mea-surEd, a "boutique global education consultancy dedicated to working with partners to collect and analyze data and improve learning for all children around the world."[*] They analyzed methods being used in India, West Africa, and East Africa to create positive collaboration and then documented the commonalities. We then set about constructing the results into a set of downloadable resources, which include an operational guide, case studies, workshops, and facilitator notes to support better collaboration and integration across national, subnational, and regional education systems.

Furthermore, Global Schools Forum and the IDP Foundation are providing small grants with tailored support for local actors to help them actualize the toolkit. It has proved to be a great success and continues to be downloaded by a remarkable number of schools and organizations globally.

GLOBAL ADVOCACY

In 2023, the Global Partnership for Education (GPE) published an article written by IDPF's CEO and my successor, Corina Gardner. Although we have had many articles published on various partner sites and news outlets, this piece was a huge victory and a clear sign that global attitudes are finally shifting around the critical role that independent, low-fee private schools play in providing education in marginalized communities underserved by public schools.

GPE plays an outsized role in shaping national education policy in low- and lower-middle-income countries, despite not being the largest funder. That title goes to the World Bank, which has the biggest education portfolio globally. GPE is funded collectively by all

---

[*] Oxford MeasurEd, "Homepage," accessed April 14, 2025, https://www.oxfordmeasured.co.uk/.

the donor governments and many big philanthropies. In a way, they are the UN for education. Their board is made up of both donor governments and recipient governments, and they have vast resources. All the money gets disbursed to the ministries of education in developing countries.

Interestingly, one of the strongest voices on the GPE board is the one seat given to civil society. For years, this group has strongly opposed the inclusion of low-fee private schools in education policy, pushing for measures that block any public funding from being allocated to support them.

So, for Corina to get an article posted on their website discussing the positive role of non-state schools in paving a way to universal education was *huge*. She was successful precisely because she made airtight arguments backed by concrete facts, which were impossible to refute. It took a huge amount of diplomacy and trust-building over the course of about eight months to get the article published.

This milestone signified the gradual acceptance of low-fee private schools in the eyes of global education stakeholders, particularly those who have traditionally fought against their existence or hosted negative or adversarial conversations. While there is still some ignorance, willful or otherwise, on low-fee private schools' vital contribution to global education systems in the developing world, there is growing acceptance of their role in SDG 4. The next step is the acceptance and inclusion of low-fee private schools in national educational policies for the greater good of a well-educated world. It has been a difficult journey, but IDPF has been instrumental in influencing this acceptance.

MOBILIZING FINANCING

In 2023, the SDG Impact Finance Initiative awarded a grant to a consortium that brought together the IDP Foundation, Global Schools Forum, Varthana, and Kaizenvest to improve access to quality education in Africa.* The SDG Impact Finance Initiative, with support from Convergence, the global network for blended finance, reviewed seventy-six applications, awarding seven with grants. The grant for this consortium's proposal was the only one awarded to an education initiative.

Since the original award, we have also partnered with Save the Children Global Ventures, and our goal is to create a US$50 million fund to focus on sub-Saharan Africa (the Generation Empowerment Fund), filtering the money into financial institutions locally, who then on-lend it to schools and other local businesses that can improve the lives of children through improved nutrition, sanitation, education, climate resilience, and health. One of the more innovative aspects of the fund design is to use blended financing (debt plus grant) to provide financial incentives to schools that can improve the literacy and numeracy rates of their students.

Part of the funding received will go to creating wraparound services, which will include hiring a firm to create an inexpensive and sustainable way of testing schools to see how they're performing through the creation of an assessment system. I will confess to some skepticism of how plausible it is to create a robust and reliable assessment system; however, I was reminded of Liesel's early admonishment

---

* Convergence, "The SDG Impact Finance Initiative Window Announces Its First Winners," January 11, 2023, https://www.convergence.finance/ news/3929YYiPLvRT1RzW9zB51Z/view.

to me when we were first starting out in Ghana all those years ago: If it was easy, someone would already have done it.

STRONGER TOGETHER

As I reflect on all the foundation has experienced over the past sixteen years—the challenges and lessons, the explorations and achievements—I think about how hard work, commitment, flexibility, and collaboration are coming to fruition. I cannot help but look back to the beginning of this journey when I realized that I was quite alone in wanting to help low-fee private schools. Wherever I went to find support, I encountered roadblocks and perceived reasons why a sustainable program of support to these schools and a shift in education systems could never work. But I persisted. Slowly I built a coalition of like-minded people, all of whom believed in these extraordinary entrepreneurs and that change was a possibility, even if getting there is full of challenges. Today, we are not only finding individuals, but we are partnering with like-minded organizations, and now we have a steady stream of people who come to us to work together to take the conversation forward.

Equally gratifying is that many other funders are joining us at the table. This allows us to leverage our work by bringing in more local partners to bring more finance into education, extend our influence, and have more local reach.

We've joined many different networks to understand how to be part of the broader conversation and work to create a collective voice representing low-fee private schools. In addition to the Global Schools Forum, which we have been supporting through its incredible growth, we can now include the Education Finance Network, International Education Funders Group (IEFG), Comparative and

International Education Society (CIES), UN Economic and Social Council (ECOSOC), UNESCO High-Level Steering Committee, Stronger Foundations for Nutrition (SFN), and the Local Education Group (LEG) in Ghana. We are invited to join more networks dedicated to impact investing and philanthropy so we can explain our approach to education financing.

Furthermore, the training program we started with Sinapi Aba has continuously been developed through various iterations over the past decade and a half, and it has the potential to extend across the continent and beyond. IDPF and Sinapi Aba went to Kenya to provide financial training expertise to three different financial institutions. They demonstrated how to administer effective proprietor training. The result is that three different financial institutions now have their own significant portfolio of low-fee private schools. This will translate into thousands of new schools being reached through financial partners who will be working from the manuals we originally created for the IDP Rising Schools Program.

We always provide the manuals to organizations free of charge, and on the agreement, they report back on how many low-fee private schools they are reaching, how often they hold training, and how many proprietors have received this training.

Where the foundation has grown to today is a testament to the determination and grit I demonstrated in our founding years. That drive allowed me to build partnerships while insisting upon creating local engagement and collaboration. At the outset, it was crucial to build partnerships and advocate at the international level to show the importance of these schools, and it was a long and arduous road that took significant time and resources. The tremendous amount of energy, work, and expertise required had led me to the decision to hire a CEO and empower the team while remaining an active board chair. Have there been bumps along the way? Of course! But I am profoundly happy with my choice, and I am thrilled and excited by the progress of the program.

EPILOGUE

I am in Ghana to celebrate the fifteen-year anniversary of the Rising Schools Program. This event is important to me, to IDPF, and to our partners. It is a beautiful evening, and so many of our friends and collaborators are here to celebrate the occasion.

After a short film extolling the work we have accomplished over the course of the past decade and a half, I am invited up onto the stage to make a few remarks. I briefly discuss the formation of the Rising Schools Program and praise the hard work of those who realized my vision. I share my deeply held belief that nations are not lifted out of poverty by receiving aid but by investing in education. I am soon joined by Tony Fosu from Sinapi Aba. He shares his memories of the early days as we drove cross-country in search of schools to ask them how we might most effectively help them. We share our mutual dream with the audience—that the children we meet be given every possible chance to achieve their dreams.

What happens next is the most moving part of the evening and the most meaningful to me. Constance Kwaa Ababio, our policy and advocacy manager, brings four alumni to the stage from our program. One is now a medical student, another is an environmental scientist, a third is a trained midwife, and the fourth is studying chemistry at university. I am proud of Constance. She does a beautiful job interviewing them. The questions are good, and the answers are comfortable and on point. These brilliant young people speak glowingly of the environment in which they received their primary education and how crucial it had been to allow them to both formulate and follow their dreams.

I am momentarily taken back to the children I first met when I visited Paulina's Queensland School. They had shared their dreams with me of being an actor, a doctor, or an astronaut, and I had been gripped by a fierce drive and passion to provide a safe environment for them to be educated so that their dreams would not just remain abstract but could be realized.

We hear from other key stakeholders, including the inestimable treasure that is Lily Baah, who has been one of the Rising Schools Program's greatest success stories. She speaks in glowing terms of her participation and how much it transformed her school and her life and helped her achieve so many of her dreams and the dreams of her pupils.

I am feeling a little overwhelmed. As praise is heaped upon Liesel and me for our work, I find that I am uncomfortable. Although I love public speaking and enjoy being in the spotlight when I have a message to deliver, being the center of attention in this way feels contrary to the way I set up the foundation and the people I intended to support. It was not ever about me but about the children and my desire to see them face the world with the advantages of a good education.

However, as I listen, I have a visceral moment in which it comes to me that some sixteen years later, all the fighting and scraping and sheer hard work has paid off. The program is not only working, but here, tonight, are beneficiaries and practitioners sharing their stories and triumphs, their gratitude for the program, and their certainty that without the resources we provided, they would still be struggling.

I go back to my first school and meet Paulina in the Agbogbloshie Market. She really was the catalyst. Without the spark she ignited in me, none of this would have happened. And look at her today. Her school is a marvelous oasis in the middle of the market. The infrastructure is sound, impressive, concrete, and massive. Classrooms are separated from each other by concrete walls, and although a little sound bleeds in from one room to the other, the children can concentrate on their studies. Her school is packed. The sounds of learning now fill the air along with the laughter and joy elicited by good teachers and a sound curriculum.

The school has toilets and plumbing. The classrooms are well lit, and gone are the terrifying hanging electrical cables. The floors and staircases are sturdy and well constructed. There is a well-stocked library and even a computer lab where the children can learn the essentials of navigating the digital age. There are still no state schools in the vicinity.

When I started out, most people, if they acknowledged that low-fee private schools existed at all, didn't believe that they were worthy of attention. When asked about low-fee private schools, their initial response was always, "Well, they shouldn't be in operation. Why would you want to help them? Why would you stand behind such an institution?"

My team and I saw the situation differently. We saw these proprietors as authentic social entrepreneurs deserving of help. We saw that what they were providing was vital to the greater macro-problem of intergenerational poverty and that we could help address this situation with the Rising Schools Program. We saw a space where the typical government or international aid agency response had been regrettably ineffective.

The model we designed didn't look like any other donor or philanthropic models or government programs in existence. It was invented from scratch, informed by a lot of intelligent, localized research gathered by sheer hard work, deep determination, and passion. The creation of the program was informed by our understanding of how microfinance works; by knowing what small-business entrepreneurs need, how they interact, and what motivates them; and most importantly, by our ability to listen and learn from the Ghanaians themselves.

By collaborating with and providing resources to Sinapi Aba, we enabled them to take a risk that has paid off to their benefit and to ours—and most of all to the benefit of school proprietors and thousands of students.

Sinapi Aba was the only partner willing to take on the risk necessary to start the Rising Schools Program. Over the past sixteen years, they have, against all odds, moved to create a sustainable program. That it is still sustainable and still providing loans is truly remarkable and a testament to their unwavering commitment to transforming the lives of the poor.

I am extraordinarily proud of my team. I have been able to slowly pull back, leaving my senior team to continue to drive my vision forward and see that the program stays true to its core values and roots. I will forever be grateful for their fortitude and engagement.

From the early days of microcredit, even as the field was expanding and being tested as a model throughout the developing world, schools were never seen as creditworthy, viable businesses. I disagreed. This is Paulina's story, in fact. After seeing her school, I said, "This school is a business, and we should be treating Paulina's school and schools like hers as businesses. We should be giving them the same level of respect that other small and midsize enterprises get."

That's just what we did. And now look at us! We've created a model that is not only sustainable but is replicated, and its widespread application, in conjunction with government programs, has massive positive implications. Now we must consider ways in which artificial intelligence (AI) for education is going to further change the landscape. We continue to keep a close eye on the evolution of the role of AI and the massive impact it is likely to have (see Appendix B). The day may come when we reach all children and achieve the goal of Education for All.

And so, as I sit upon the stage and look up at the Ghanaian night sky and breathe in the event underway around me, I suddenly am forced to recognize that I have done something meaningful with my life. I am doing something that matters. And it feels good!

STANDING AT THE EDGE
OF CHANGE

Corina Gardner, CEO, IDP Foundation, Inc.

As this book is being published, the international development sector is facing a seismic shift—one that will reshape everything across aid, philanthropy, and power.

By the time you read this, the future may already look very different. Across the globe, major funders are pulling back. USAID funding is frozen. Aid budgets across Europe are shrinking. And for the first time in a long time, it's clear that donor countries will no longer be in a position to inappropriately shape priorities on behalf of recipients.

Many in our field have been pushing for this shift for years. We've called for "localization," for power to move into the hands of the communities we serve. But real change is often slow—until it's not. When necessity steps in, systems that once seemed immovable can suddenly collapse.

The cracks are showing. The old models of development, where funders dictate terms and communities have little say, are no longer sustainable.

At the IDP Foundation, we have been preparing for this moment for a long time. In fact, we were built for it.

Unlike much of traditional development programming, the IDP Foundation has always worked from the ground up. From the beginning, we chose a different path—one led by local demand, not donor agendas. Our work supporting already established low-fee private schools, our investment in sustainable financing models, and our commitment to entrepreneurship and education have all been designed to reflect the reality on the ground, not theories from afar.

We didn't create parallel systems. We strengthened what already existed. We listened first. We prioritized financial sustainability, because true empowerment means communities shouldn't have to rely on foreign aid forever.

And we've stayed focused on the long game: shifting intergenerational poverty through education and entrepreneurship.

Now, as the sector grapples with uncertainty, I believe our model is more relevant, and more necessary, than ever.

We know it's possible to be locally led and financially sustainable. We know it's possible to build lasting change without creating dependency. We've seen it in action. And we believe it's time to share these lessons more widely—to demonstrate that a different way forward is not only possible but urgent.

Of course, we don't have all the answers. No one does. And in times like these, humility is just as important as innovation.

As funders, we must continue to ask ourselves hard questions:

- Are we using grants wisely, or could investments achieve the same outcomes while stretching resources further?
- Are we doing enough to support collaboration and consolidation among local actors rather than forcing competition?
- Are we willing to align reporting requirements, commingle unrestricted funding, and invest in public goods that lift all boats, including private actors?
- Are we truly shifting power, or just shifting language?

This is the work ahead. It will be messy. It will be imperfect. It will require us to stay open, curious, and brave enough to change course when needed.

But one thing is clear: The old ways are ending. And if we want to build something better, we must be willing to flip the market right-side up—to ensure that those who live the realities we seek to change are the ones setting the demand.

At the IDP Foundation, this has always been our North Star. And as we move forward into a future that is anything but certain, it will continue to guide us.

Because real change doesn't start with us. It starts with listening.

IDP Foundation, Inc.
INNOVATION · DEVELOPMENT · PROGRESS

SCAN THE QR CODE BELOW
OR VISIT IDPFOUNDATION.ORG
TO LEARN MORE ABOUT THE
IDP FOUNDATION AND STAY
UPDATED ON OUR MISSION,
PROGRAMS, AND IMPACT.

APPENDIX A

The 2008 United Nations Millennium Development Goals (MDGs) aimed to be achieved by 2015 were replaced by the Sustainable Development Goals (SDGs), which were much more comprehensive and aimed to be achieved by 2030.

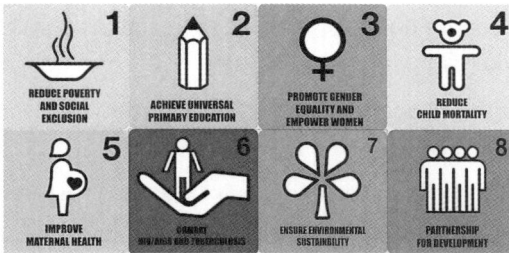

SUSTAINABLE DEVELOPMENT GOALS*

Goal 1. End poverty in all its forms everywhere.

Goal 2. End hunger, achieve food security and improved nutrition, and promote sustainable agriculture.

Goal 3. Ensure healthy lives and promote well-being for all at all ages.

Goal 4. Ensure inclusive and equitable quality education, and promote lifelong learning opportunities for all.

Goal 5. Achieve gender equality and empower all women and girls.

Goal 6. Ensure availability and sustainable management of water and sanitation for all.

Goal 7. Ensure access to affordable, reliable, sustainable, and modern energy for all.

Goal 8. Promote sustained, inclusive, and sustainable economic growth, full and productive employment, and decent work for all.

Goal 9. Build resilient infrastructure, promote inclusive and sustainable industrialization, and foster innovation.

Goal 10. Reduce inequality within and among countries.

Goal 11. Make cities and human settlements inclusive, safe, resilient, and sustainable.

Goal 12. Ensure sustainable consumption and production patterns.

Goal 13. Take urgent action to combat climate change and its impacts.

Goal 14. Conserve and sustainably use the oceans, seas and marine resources for sustainable development.

Goal 15. Protect, restore, and promote sustainable use of terrestrial ecosystems, sustainably manage forests, combat desertification, and halt and reverse land degradation and halt biodiversity loss.

Goal 16. Promote peaceful and inclusive societies for sustainable development, provide access to justice for all and build effective, accountable, and inclusive institutions at all levels.

Goal 17. Strengthen the means of implementation and revitalize the Global Partnership for Sustainable Development.

---

* If you want to learn more about the United Nations Sustainable Development Goals, visit un.org/sustainable-development-goals. The content of this book has not been approved by the United Nations and does not reflect the views of the United Nations or its officials or member states.

APPENDIX B
Learning in the Age of AI

If we teach today's students as we taught yesterday's, we rob them of tomorrow.

—John Dewey

ROMANA KROPILOVA, DIRECTOR OF EDTECH, AI-FOR-EDUCATION.ORG

In a corner of the dusty classroom in Greater Accra, eight-year-old Kwasi is holding a smartphone and reading a sentence in English. Others in the room are engaged in an English lesson with Madam Erica. It is her ninth year as a teacher at this school. A few minutes later, Kwasi stands up and walks back to his seat. His neighbor Nana jumps up eagerly and walks to the back of the room, taking the phone from the desk with excitement. She enjoys using the smartphone. They are the last two in the class to do a short reading assessment with the help of voice AI.

Shortly after they are done, the class is over and the students have a break. Most of them run outside energetically even if it is a hot day in the middle of the dry season called *harmattan*. Madam Erica, feeling the heat of the day, takes a few breaths. Her commute this morning in the packed local tro tro minibus took nearly two hours because of traffic. She slowly collects the phone, and as she looks at the display, she can't help but smile. In a color-coded dashboard, she can see the results of the assessment and the students grouped by reading levels. More than a third of the forty-one students in her class made very good progress since the last assessment just a couple of weeks ago. She can also see recommendations for exercises for the different levels in class.

As a seasoned teacher, she was skeptical about this new tool at first, but after the training she received a couple of months ago and the discussions with coaches through the peer WhatsApp group chat, she learned to like it. "So good this works without consuming data," she thinks to herself before she walks out into the courtyard.

While this is not a true story, it is far from science fiction. In fact, automatic speech recognition (ASR) is being used to support formative assessment of the reading skills in several low- and middle-income countries (LMICs) already, such as in India and Brazil. And Ghana too has tested AI-powered edtech with some promising results.

The speed of the recent developments of generative AI is mind-blowing, and everything points to a future where it is part of our daily lives. As Mustafa Suleyman, the author of the book *The Coming Wave*, writes: "Almost every foundational technology ever invented, from pickaxes to plows, pottery to photography, phones to planes, and everything in between, follows a single, seemingly immutable law: it gets cheaper and easier to use, and ultimately it proliferates, far and wide." History confirms this pattern, suggesting that AI is on the same path.

If that is the case, how can we ensure that every learner benefits from this powerful technology and that it doesn't deepen existing divides? In the sections that follow, I suggest some of the areas in which AI can make a difference in the LMICs' contexts and what roadblocks we need to overcome to fully realize its promise.

KEY AREAS OF IMPACT

While AI could transform the way we approach education in the long term, there are already key areas where it has impact today. These can be grouped based on who the technology is supporting: teachers, system-level actors, and students.

Supporting Teachers

The teachers everywhere, and even more in the LMICs, have a noble profession—and an extremely challenging one. One of the realities LMIC educators need to grapple with is big classrooms, often exceeding fifty students in sub-Saharan Africa. Pre-service training and ongoing professional development opportunities are limited in many places. Formative assessment and lesson planning are two areas where AI can be an enabler and support the day-to-day of teachers.

Formative assessment is an ongoing process used during learning to provide feedback and guide instruction, rather than just evaluating final outcomes. It has been extensively studied and recognized as a tool to enhance learning. As in the example of reading skills at the beginning of this section, AI can help teachers with automating the assessment process and grading. Moreover, it can make suggestions on instruction based on the results. This could mean grouping students according to their level and sharing different exercises.

Lesson planning is another area where AI can assist teachers by providing resources and strategies. The Oak National Academy in the UK has developed Aila, an AI-powered lesson planning assistant with contextual curriculum alignment for teachers. The findings from their annual 2024 independent impact evaluation show that their users work five or more hours less per week. Seventy-three percent of users reported a positive impact on workload. Interestingly, the tool is used more in disadvantaged areas, when measured by income. These kinds of solutions have been implemented in different contexts already. Another promising example is Escola Nova in Brazil, whose lessons are accessed by nearly a million teachers monthly. They achieved a Net Promoter Score (NPS) of over eighty-eight and scored above nine out of ten on quality assessments. How? They offer a comprehensive repository of lesson plans across various subjects and grade levels aligned with the national curriculum, developed over several years and being continually improved together with experienced educators.

An important takeaway from implementing programs with education technology (edtech) is that the distribution of devices or tools alone is not enough. Carefully designed complementary measures, including teacher training on how to use the tools, are needed to create an impact.

Supporting System-Level Actors

Then, there are the system-level actors in education at the meso and macro levels. These range from school leaders and district administrators to national policymakers, curriculum developers, and those responsible for teacher training and edtech. On all these levels, AI can facilitate their work, give timely access to actionable insights, and improve the quality of the decisions.

More concretely, AI can support these education stakeholders by analyzing large volumes of education data such as student assessments, teacher allocation, school infrastructure, or budget distribution. For example, AI-powered dashboards can help ministries identify regions with declining literacy outcomes or schools that may need additional support. AI tools can also enhance monitoring and evaluation by automating data collection, synthesizing large datasets, and surfacing trends in real time. It is fascinating that it is possible now to analyze thousands of school reports or teacher surveys almost instantly, providing an overview of key trends and actionable insights. This is exciting because it allows for faster feedback loops and adjustment of implementation based on evidence.

One of AI's most promising roles is in providing localized, contextualized support, especially in linguistically and culturally diverse systems like those that can be found in sub-Saharan Africa. For instance, Nigeria alone is home to over five thousand languages! AI can help translate and adapt educational content into local languages, ensuring no one is left behind because of language or location—for a fraction of the cost that standard methods would require. A great example is RobotsMali, a nonprofit organization which used a combination of ChatGPT, machine translation, and human editors to produce more than 180 culturally relevant children's books in Bambara, one of Mali's most spoken languages. They even created images to accompany the text, and this all took them less than a year. This demonstrates how AI can enable culturally relevant learning materials to be produced quickly and affordably.

Supporting Students

Last but definitely not least, AI holds a big promise for personalization and tutoring. It can be a learning companion for students, and tools like LearnLM, developed by Google, give us a taste of what the future might look like. Grounded in educational research, LearnLM doesn't just provide all the answers—it can act like a tutor and guide the students through the learning process. Just imagine how this can transform the test preparation or the opportunities for self-directed learning.

It is listed last here because in many LMICs, the structural barriers to large-scale implementation of personalized AI solutions remain the highest, such as limited access to devices, connectivity, and infrastructure. Nevertheless, there are promising examples of adaptation to the local context. One of them is EIDU, a platform providing interactive learning content via low-cost mobile phones, working in offline settings. Operating effectively already with one device per classroom, EIDU has managed to keep costs low while reaching over 390,000 learners to date. A one-year randomized controlled trial by EdTech Hub examining the personalized learning solution from EIDU provided preliminary data showing significant improvement in learning outcomes among students using the tool. The study indicates that using EIDU in schools can add the equivalent of 0.8 years of learning development.

These examples showcase how AI can support education at different levels when it is thoughtfully implemented. However, to make the most of AI's capabilities in education, we need to address some of the important structural and ethical challenges that currently stand in the way of equitable implementation.

TOWARD EQUITABLE AI

As exciting as these technological innovations are, it is still the reality today that—according to a World Bank Group report—by the age of ten, nine out of ten children in sub-Saharan Africa are unable to read and understand a simple text, despite the progress in school enrollment. This is a reminder that access alone is not enough. The question then is: What needs to happen for AI tools to help the education systems leapfrog the learning poverty?

While education systems are complex and each context brings its unique challenges, there are three key barriers that we need to collectively address for AI to make a positive difference in LMICs.

1. AI-powered solutions reflect global disparities.

Most of the foundational AI large language models are trained on data coming from high-income countries. The data coming from LMIC context is scarce. To put it in perspective, a US AI Safety Institute report shows that less than half of one percent of the data used to train large AI models comes from Africa, despite the continent representing almost one-fifth of the global population.

What's needed:
- Multistakeholder collaboration to co-create locally relevant solutions and to learn from similar contexts. This includes partnerships across governments, researchers, NGOs, tech providers, and local communities.
- Building more diverse data to train AI models by adding existing data that is not digitized in a format that works for training the large language models and by collecting new data from regions that are not well represented. This is crucial to

have solutions that work for every learner and do not discriminate based on where the learners are from, their accent, or their gender.

2. **Solutions are not designed with systemwide implementation in mind.**

A lot of the local innovation is happening in small-scale projects with unclear paths to scale and without clear evidence of what works.

What's needed:
- Designing solutions with the available infrastructure and cost-effectiveness in mind. The offline-first curriculum-aligned resources created by Learning Equality are a good example. Early partnerships with governments are critical to embed these innovations into public systems.
- Rethinking how we generate and use evidence. Considering the pace at which AI models develop, we need to consider how we measure and assess quality both for inputs and outputs. That also means new ways to assess the quality and performance of the AI models themselves, like the benchmarks created by AI-for-Education.org, as well as faster loops for implementation research to identify what works, for whom, and under what conditions.

3. **AI in education lacks unified policies on ethics and child protection.**

As AI enters the classroom, ethical safeguards must evolve in parallel. Without clear guidance, there's a risk of compromising children's privacy, safety, and rights.

What's needed:
- Develop and continually update ethical frameworks specific to AI in education, grounded in child protection and digital rights.
- Balance innovation with protection, ensuring learners are not exposed to harm while enabling creativity and progress.

Addressing these barriers can ensure that the use of AI-powered tools leads to more equitable, impactful, and safe learning experiences.

• • •

Education plays an important role in preparing children to become responsible, active, and considerate members of society. Technologies like AI can offer support by enhancing teachers' effectiveness and making learning more personalized, inclusive, and grounded in local realities and evidence. If implemented with these considerations in mind, AI can serve as a helpful assistant, allowing educators like

Madam Erica to focus on what matters most: the human interactions and relationships that are essential for meaningful learning.

AI is no longer a distant future—it's already here, and it's here to stay. The opportunity before us is to shape and guide this technology so it empowers educators and system-level actors and reaches every learner, regardless of where they live. Now is the time to embrace this powerful innovation together so that every child, like Kwasi and Nana, has the chance to achieve their full potential and thrive.

APPENDIX C
Original IDP Rising Schools
Program Questionnaire

During the development of the Rising Schools Program, gathering feedback and actively listening to school proprietors was a crucial step in understanding the challenges they faced and identifying the financial literacy and school management support they needed to succeed with school loans.

As of June 2025, US$1 roughly equaled GHS₵10. At the height of the currency devaluation of the Ghanaian cedi, US$1 equaled GHS₵16. The value of the Ghanaian cedi against the US dollar is improving, which is due to a multitude of variables, including the recent devaluation of the US dollar along with increased stability in the Ghanaian economy.

The letter that follows was shared with the proprietors who participated, along with the questionnaires.

IDP FOUNDATION, INC.

Irene D. Pritzker
President

October 2008

Dear School Owner:

First – a big congratulations to you for starting a school for children who desperately need your help.

Below is a long questionnaire that will help us to better understand your needs and enable us to try to help you with your goal of establishing a self sustaining school that will serve many poor children. Because of your heart and efforts in educating the poor, you are in a position to change their whole future.

What you are doing is indeed noble, and we hope that we will find a way to help you fulfill your dreams and those of so many young people.

This questionnaire is confidential and your name and your school will not be shared with anyone other than Sinapi Aba Trust, Opportunity International and the IDP Foundation.

This questionnaire is not meant to judge your school. It is simply to find out about it. In order to help you, we need to know the problems you are facing, and what you most need in order for your school to be able to get a micro finance loan and become able to pay for itself. That is why you must be very truthful in filling out this questionnaire otherwise we will not really know what you truly need and how we might go about best trying to help you.

We know we are asking a lot of questions. We have done that in order that you can give short answers, although we will give you space to add anything else you would like to add at the end.

Please try to answer all the questions as honestly and thoughtfully as possible. If there is a question that doesn't fit your school, then just write N/A in the answer space.

This was a highly comprehensive questionnaire. Building on my original set of sixty-five questions, we expanded it to about one hundred questions. Below are excerpts showcasing typical responses from school proprietors:

<u>**General Questions:**</u>

1. Why did you decide to begin a school?
   - Proprietor has always dreamt of being in the Private Sector.
   - He realised that the government has a huge burden on education. So he beginning a school could ease the burden.
   - He also begun a school because he wanted wanted to provide employment for all.

Who are the students? Where do they come from?

The students are children within the community.
they come from the community.
These are children of teachers, traders and farmers.

How many grade levels does your school currently have?

~~KG~~ Nursery, KG1, KG2, Primary 1 - 5.

How many students were there in your school when you started it? **4**

Who are the parents of your students? Do they work close by, and how many of them have reliable incomes? Please try to give as much information, in a general sense, as you know about the typical situations of the parents of your students.

The parents of ~~th~~ his students are mostly farmers, petty traders and teacher. They work in the community. ~~#~~ Most of them have reliable incomes. because they are able to pay their fees by the close of the term.

Is there a government school close enough for your students to attend if they wished? Yes

Why do you think that their parents prefer that they come to your school instead of the government school?

− Academic work is good.
− People consider his school accessible in terms of proximity from their homes to school.
− The children are also treated with care

Do you teach the state set curriculum in your school?

Yes.

Do you have any training in how to run a business?

No

How do you go about getting teaching aids for your school?

Proprietor buys them.

Does your school have a PTA? If so, what role do they play?

Yes. The PTA discuss issues concerning the School.

Do you have enough text books for each student? No

How do you discipline students that misbehave?

− Students who misbehave are detained during break and are sometimes sup suspended from School

Do your students pay fees? Yes.

If so, how much do they pay? Please tell us the payment arrangements. Do they pay per term? Do they pay per day? Do they pay per week?

KG 1 to 2   GH¢ 5.00   per term.
Pim 1 – 6   GH¢ 6.00   per term
JHS   GH¢ 8.00   per term.

What does their payment cover? Tell us anything that parents must pay for that tuition/school fees do not cover. For example, although we have already asked about uniforms and food and water, please list again in this section how much you charge for food and water if you provide those things. Also tell us how you collect for any extra charges other than school fees. *(Interviewer may ask about: feeding, transportation, registration, uniform, textbook, printing, extra class, sports, or any other fees/charges).*

Canteen – GH¢ 0.30 or 0.40p daily.
registration – GH¢ 5.00
printing   – GH¢ 1.00 to GH¢ 2.00
Extra classes – GH¢ 0.10 daily
Sports   – GH¢ 0.50 per term.
medical fees – GH¢ 0.50 per term.

Do you have any financial support for your school other than school fees from the students who are attending? Yes.
Propri Proprietor has taken loan from SAT
– Proprietor uses other business to subsidize School

Do you have any formal training in accounting? No

Do you know how to create a balance sheet and a cash flow statement?

No

. What are your school's expenses? *(Interviewer note: ask about salaries, food, books, rent, transportation, electricity, water, other expenses).*

Salaries GH¢ 30 - 55   - monthly.

Food   GH¢ 300   - every two weeks

books   GH¢ 100   - yearly.

Water   GH¢ 20   - monthly.

medical   GH¢ 20   - termly.

ACKNOWLEDGMENTS

Alone we can do so little;
together we can do so much.

—Helen Keller

In this limited space, it's impossible to thank all of the hundreds of people who helped bring this story to life.

First, I must thank my daughter, Liesel, who placed her trust in me to lead the IDPF and choose this path.

I'm deeply grateful to the entire IDPF team—past and present—and especially to our current leadership: Corina Gardner, Stephen Caleb Opuni, Raphael Akomeah, and Alison Ehlke. Special thanks to Alison, who over the past fourteen years has not only kept me on track but also ensured everything around me kept moving forward. I'm also thankful for Allison Lawshe, our former program manager, whose tireless dedication left a lasting and meaningful impact.

And I'm grateful to Michael Halberstam for his dedication to this book and for making the journeys to Ghana and Kenya to conduct so many thoughtful interviews with the remarkable individuals whose voices shape this story. Much gratitude also to my personal assistant, Tiffany Meier, for her desperate attempts to keep me organized.

A special thanks to my Ghanaian partners, particularly Tony Fosu and Vincent Amponsah of Sinapi Aba, for their steadfast partnership and shared commitment, and to my many friends in the Ghana Education Service and Ghana Ministry of Education over these many years. My gratitude to Professor Damasus Tuuro-song, president of the Ghana National Association of Private Schools (GNAPS). Thank you also to Victor King Anyanful of the Center for Professional Development, Training, and Education (CPDTE) and Simon Graffy of Inspiring Teachers, who are leading to groundbreaking improvements in literacy and numeracy. And thanks to Patrick Awuah, founder and president of Ashesi University for his inspirational leadership.

To the many school proprietors—thank you for your perseverance and unwavering commitment. Despite limited resources, you have worked tirelessly to educate thousands of children and build brighter futures. Thanks in particular to Paulina Nlando and the other school owners mentioned specifically in the book—Lily Baah, Paa Willie, and Magdalene Sackey— for sharing their inspirational stories. Thanks also to Franklin Cudjoe, founder of Imani, a think tank in Ghana.

Thank you to James Tooley, whose lecture and documentary about his work intrigued me and ultimately provided direction for the whole IDP Foundation.

A heartfelt thank you to Opportunity International for inviting me on my first trip to Ghana—a journey I never could have imag-ined would lead us to where we are today.

Thanks to consultants Peter Colenso and Sham Sandhu for their effective guidance, to Andy Sprunger (who was instrumental in creating the Rising Schools Program training manuals), to Raza Jafar for his strategic advice, to Okendo Lewis-Gayle for introducing me to Harambeans, and to Romana Kropilova, director of edtech at AI-for-Education.org.

Special thanks to Amir Dossal, former executive director of the United Nations Office for Partnerships, for his personal guidance and for opening almost every door imaginable within the UN. His support has been invaluable, and I am deeply grateful. Irina Bokova, former director-general of UNESCO, deserves credit for giving me a global platform to share my story, as does Luce Brigham, chief of office at UNOP. And thanks to Elizabeth Littlefield, former CEO of the Overseas Private Investment Corporation (now the US Development Finance Corporation), for her wise guidance in how to shape the foundation's direction.

Thanks to Bob Hercules and the team at Media Process Group and filmmaker Jonathan Olinger of HUMAN for beautifully capturing the essence of the Rising Schools Program through photographs and films. And it would be remiss of me not to mention our partnership with Sesame Workshop and the creation of the fourteen Muppet videos; this was a thoroughly memorable and fun experience.

Much gratitude to Synergos, who in the early days provided connections that have proven to be long-lasting and invaluable.

Thank you to the many friends and colleagues who generously read early drafts of this book and offered invaluable feedback.

To the team at Amplify Publishing, including project manager Brandon Coward, editor Rebecca Andersen, designer Josh Taggert, and CEO Naren Aryal—thank you for your great work helping to bring this book to life.

ABOUT THE AUTHOR

Irene Pritzker cofounded the IDP Foundation, Inc., with her daughter, Liesel, in 2008. She was motivated when she visited Ghana that same year and saw how many local schools had barely any infrastructure or resources. Irene considered whether it would be possible to successfully provide a business loan to these schools given that they had no collateral but were serving the poorest families in Ghana.

Focusing on localization and working closely with government, the school proprietors, and an extraordinary microfinance NGO, Sinapi Aba, she launched a successful pilot program. The program continues to grow today and is no longer dependent on aid. The model has been replicated, expanding with new partners into new countries, reaching over 2,300 schools, and serving over 500,000 children.

In addition to program development, Irene actively works to mission-align the foundation's investment strategy—particularly incorporating alignment with the Sustainable Development Goals. The foundation has also made significant contributions to extraordinary developments in medical research.

As an advocate for developing sustainable and market-driven solutions that are no longer aid-dependent, Irene has frequently been invited to share the work of her philosophy behind the IDP Rising Schools Program. She has given major speeches on effective philanthropic investment and participated in numerous panels at the United Nations and other international forums, including throughout the US, Accra, Beijing, Paris, Zurich, Istanbul, Rome, and Dubai.

She has won multiple awards, including the American Association for Cancer Research Public Service Award, the Foreign Policy Association Global Philanthropy Award, and the Australian Consul-General's Outstanding Achievement Award. In 2012 the IDP Foundation, Inc., was granted special consultative status to the United Nations, which continues to this day.